T0072329

Through It

50 Devotions

for

Difficult Journeys

Dana C. Branson, PhD, LCSW

WESTBOW
PRESS®
A DIVISION OF THOMAS NELSON
& ZONDERVAN

This book is a work of non-fiction. Unless otherwise noted, the author and the publisher make no explicit guarantees as to the accuracy of the information contained in this book and in some cases, names of people and places have been altered to protect their privacy.

WestBow Press books may be ordered through booksellers or by contacting:

WestBow Press
A Division of Thomas Nelson & Zondervan
1663 Liberty Drive
Bloomington, IN 47403
www.westbowpress.com
844-714-3454

Unless otherwise indicated, scripture quotations are taken from the Holy Bible, New International Version®, NIV®. Copyright © 1973, 1978, 1984 by Biblica, Inc.™ Used by permission of Zondervan. All rights reserved worldwide.

Scripture quotations marked ESV are from the ESV Bible® (The Holy Bible, English Standard Version®), copyright © 2001 by Crossway Bibles, a publishing ministry of Good News Publishers. Used by permission. All rights reserved.

ISBN: 979-8-3850-0748-6 (sc)
ISBN: 979-8-3850-0749-3 (e)

Library of Congress Control Number: 2023917711

Print information available on the last page.

WestBow Press rev. date: 11/07/2023

To Alan, AJ, and Noah ... my greatest blessings.

Don't waste the storms of your life.

—Pastor Jason Reynolds
Sea of Galilee
05/25/2023

Contents

Acceptance

Shock and Denial

No Stinking Thinking

Anger

Injustice, "Why Me," and Pity Pot

Sadness

Fear, Worry, and Going Mad

Preface

In writing this book, I learned that the preface is a place for the author to tell the reader how the book came into being and why. Well, if I am being honest, this book was written due to my desperation to keep my sanity, but as it unfolded, there began a growing hope that perhaps this project could encourage someone else.

If you proceed to read this book, what you will learn is that I've had cancer twice. The first time, I was twenty-six years old. I was diagnosed with Hodgkin lymphoma, and I took on cancer, chemo, and the loveliness that goes with it like a champ. But when I was diagnosed with breast cancer at forty-nine years old, I wasn't such a good sport. There were lots of things that might have accounted for the difference between cancer 1.0 and cancer 2.0. I could blame COVID-19, the changes in the medical community from the 1990s to 2020s, the general apathy breast cancer seems to get these days since it is, thankfully, not the killer it used to be, or because, as a veteran of cancer, I knew what I was in for when I was diagnosed a second time. But the real reason I struggled is because of me. I did things differently and not in a good way. I relied far too much on myself and my own ideas of what I needed to do to be successful with adversity. I didn't do what I should have done, which was thrown myself at the feet of God and allowed him to take me through this event.

"Footprints in the Sand" is a poem / short story that lots of people have read, about a man who had a vision one night about walking on the beach with God. He noticed that there were two sets of footprints in the sand throughout his life, but during the worst times—his very darkest, there was only one set. The man questions God, "How could you have left me when I needed you most?" And God reveals that it was in these times that he carried the man (Loughead 1892). If you haven't read the poem, I highly recommend it. I know what it is like to be carried. During my first round with cancer, I was nestled safely in God's arms. I knew that I was being carried, and although it was terrible and scary, it was also an amazing place to be. Second time around, well … God was there with his arms open wide for me to jump in for another ride, but my anger and negativity wouldn't allow me to see it. Instead, I missed the opportunity to again experience that inexplicable peace and safety among daunting times. This is a story of someone who was too stubborn for her own good, and how she put herself through a whole lot of extra trouble and pain because she wouldn't move past her pride and ask for some help.

This book contains some biblical truths, positive goodness, and God-breathed directives; and then there are the examples of what *not* to do. What qualifies me to write this book? I have educational accolades, years of experience in mental health service provision, and lots of initials at the end of my name, but that really doesn't mean much. As a social worker, I can provide people with sound clinical direction, but that doesn't mean I am going to naturally follow it myself. Social workers are like compasses. We can't tell you where to go, but we can point you in the right direction.

Initially, I started this book to try to get myself back on the right track and moving in a healthier direction. But as the writing and time went along, I began to hope that it could serve a purpose and help someone else. I certainly want something productive to come out of all this, something that will honor God. I am not like the women I admire who love Jesus with a passion that oozes and drips off them. I can only aspire to shine with Jesus's love like they do. But this is my attempt to take God's love and message, mixed with some good old social work know-how, and provide some encouragement to others. Proverbs 19:21 says, "Many are the plans in a person's heart, but it is the Lord's purpose that prevails." I hope that is what you find in this book.

Acknowledgments

Anyone who knows me recognizes the need for an acknowledgment page. There is no way that I could take a book from idea to publication without a great deal of help. So here it goes, my list of thank yous.

To Michael "Mickey" Heath and his coworkers at the Writing Lab at Southeast Missouri State University. He is the man who takes my writing, edits it, and makes me look like a real writer. He has been doing this for years now and is one of the reasons that a kid who was threatened all through second grade with being retained is now a tenured professor. I am so grateful for your skill set, encouragement, and willingness to do this because you love what you do.

To Morgan Sides, for being a small-basket friend and taking in all the carnage with an "I've seen worse" face. I appreciate you more than you will ever know. God gave me a sister in you at just the right time.

To Desiree Malam, an amazing woman of God and trained professional who heard me—*really* heard me—and had the insight to say some things I needed to hear.

To my father, a fountain of wisdom, knowledge, and advice. I am grateful for your example of how to deal with adversity through quiet humility, reflection, and trust in God.

To my children, AJ and Noah, who have seen their mother through many life events. Thank you for just being kids and treating me like a mom. The best job I have ever had and ever will.

To Alan, my precious husband, thank you for running these life-event marathons with me. There is no one else I would want with me on these journeys—and likely no one else who would do it.

To the one. Thank you for my many blessings, your grace, and your mercy. Thank you too for being God and not human like the rest of us, or you would have walked away from me a *long* time ago.

Introduction

As a university professor, I read a lot of textbooks. They usually come with a section titled "How to Use This Book." It is the textbook company's way of telling you how to use the book as effectively as possible, because they know satisfied professors will request the next edition when it comes out for their students to purchase. So here it is, your "How to Use This Book" section.

What is the best way to use this book? Well, that depends entirely on you and your needs. The book is set up with ten different categories and five devotions under each category. The sections and devotions are stand-alone and can be read in any order. I envision the reader going to whatever section they need for what they are struggling with in that moment. If you are struggling with anger, there is a section for that. If you are sick and tired of being angry and want to focus on something more positive, there are sections for that too. You get to decide how you read this book. You certainly can go cover to cover, but feel free to move around and find what speaks to you. The verses come from the New International Version (NIV) of the Bible, unless otherwise identified. If you have a translation you like better, please feel free to look up the verses in your copy of God's Word and glean the truth waiting there for you.

The adversity that I write most about is cancer, as this is what provided the fodder, angst, and inspiration for the book. However, you can substitute whatever your struggle is in place of cancer. Adversity is adversity, and it has the power to make you stronger, sharpen you, and grow you like no other. It can also take you to terrible places with few redeeming qualities and turn you into someone you don't even recognize. But here is the good news—you're the one who gets to decide. It's not magical; it is intentional. It's not easy either; you have to be purposeful and strategic in your decisions, the cognitions you entertain, and how you handle emotions. What follows are a collection of devotions and journal prompts that can point you in a positive direction with biblical backup. I sincerely hope it helps you with your journey or assists you with someone else who is struggling. The journaling is optional, but this is often a catalyst for lasting and meaningful insight. Therefore, I encourage you to give it a try. Like anything else in life, you will get out of this book what you put into it. Remember, you are going for progress and growth, not perfection or complete resolution. Those things rarely happen. We are lifelong learners of ourselves and our spiritual journey—embrace the education.

1

Intentional Growth

POSTTRAUMATIC GROWTH

Posttraumatic growth (PTG) is a term coined by Drs. Tedeschi and Calhoun (1996) to describe a purposeful, cognitive, and intentional approach to trauma that allows the survivor to find personal growth. It's the professional term for taking life's lemons and making sweet lemonade! And isn't this what we all want? To go through a terrible life event and to come out stronger on the other side; to inspire others; to not be the bitter, ugly-acting, permanently damaged person who people whisper about, saying things like, "They were never the same after _____"? Yes, PTG is the way to go, but it is also a hard way to go. It's not natural. As humans, we don't embrace trauma or adversity. We're built for survival, and when something threatens our survival—physically, emotionally, cognitively, socially, and/or spiritually—we have an automatic reaction system. Growing and celebrating what we can glean from a terrible life event are not things most of us aspire to do while we are in the middle of it. In retrospect, maybe—but not while you are in the belly of the beast and feel like you are losing the fight, one painstaking blow after another.

PTG is a goal, not so much a destination. Humans are emotional beings whose capacity for logic does not fully develop until we are well into adulthood. Want proof? Think back to high school (I know … I just threw up a little in my mouth too). Remember how high school romance or friendship drama could make or break your day? When a love relationship ended and you couldn't eat or sleep, and every song you heard echoed your feelings of heartbreak as if your world had ended? Fast-forward ten years, and relationship issues are still hard and can evoke strong feelings—but we can compartmentalize. We're older, more mature; we have enough logical thinking to be able to conclude that while we might have a right to be sad, hurt, and/or angry, we also have jobs, daily life responsibilities, and other stuff to do. We move forward and do what we need to do because life stops for no one's tragedies—*no one's*!

This is where PTG can come in and make a significant difference. While Tedeschi and Calhoun get the credit for the term *PTG*, Christ came up with this philosophy much, much earlier:

> Consider it pure joy, my brothers and sisters, whenever you face trials of many kinds, because you know that the testing of your faith produces perseverance. Let perseverance finish its work so that you may be mature and complete, not lacking anything. (James 1:2–4)

Lots of us know these verses and depend on their message; there is a good reason for all this toil and trouble, and if you play your cards right, you can come out better in the end. If there was anyone in the Bible who embraced PTG, it was the apostle Paul. Among other things, Paul suffered multiple beatings and a stoning at Lystra; he was shipwrecked, set adrift at sea, and robbed; he experienced hunger, thirst, cold, hot, and nakedness; and he faced physical exhaustion and mental illness—all while knowing his life was in constant danger from his own compatriots and sworn enemies. Oh … and let's not forget that he was beheaded. Now, did Paul ever have a bad day where he was not feeling the PTG? I'm certain he did. Actually, there are many passages where Paul talks about his desire to suffer well and live a sinless life but comes up short— just like the rest of us. Romans 7:15 says, "I do not understand what I do. For what I want to do I do not do, but what I hate I do." Thank you, God, for grace anew every day. I for one need it every day, all day—and then some.

Journal Prompts

1. How do you want to *do* this time in your life? How do you want to end up (physically, emotionally, cognitively, socially, spiritually)?
2. If all things work together for the good, what good do you hope will come out of your personal trials?
3. What are three Bible verses or sayings that you can memorize, paraphrase, or write down that will help you stay in the mind frame you want?

2

Intentional Growth

NOT FEELING IT TODAY

I have a person in my life who has held many roles. At first, she was a client, then a coworker, then one of my supervisees, and now a friend and personal hero. Her name is Wanda,[1] and she has been *through it*! She suffered horrendous abuse as a child, being raised in a satanic cult, and has experienced great trauma and loss. Her path involved substance use, sex work, homelessness, prison, an unidentified long-term illness, and much more. I cannot comprehend the nightmares and tortures she has journeyed, and saying, "It's not fair," is such an understatement that's it's not worth uttering. However, Wanda was able to take her story and turn it into something that could help and heal others. Like most people, her journey to recovery is ongoing, and it has not occurred in a straight line, but she now serves as a substance-use disorder counselor, sobriety sponsor, conference speaker, and mentor to many—including me.

Have you heard the phrase "I woke up on the wrong side of the bed this morning"? As a substance-use disorder counselor, Wanda used to provide group treatment and had a group devoted to the concept of waking up on the wrong side of the bed. We have all been there. For whatever reason, you wake up and are not in a good mood. Maybe it is a physical illness or mental health issue rearing its ugly head; you didn't get enough sleep; you're dealing with difficulties in your life or

---

[1] My friend's name has been changed here to protect anonymity. I chose the name Wanda after Yadier Molina's wife—you're welcome, Wanda.

had a fight before you went to bed; your hormones are acting up, or the sun and moon are parked in the wrong spot for your particular mojo. Whatever the reason, you are not in a good place, and you have the entire day ahead of you. What do you do? Well, you can take a page out of Wanda's playbook. Get back into bed (literally, under the covers, head on the pillow, and snuggle up) and then get back up and exit the other side of the bed. If you know Wanda well, you know that she sleeps with her bed to the wall—it's a safety and security issue for her. Therefore, this means exiting the other side of the bed for her is inconvenient and difficult. But it is a physical activity to create a change in perception. It serves as an explicit moment in time where Wanda consciously decides to change her thinking. That is deliberate and purposeful … that is intentional growth. Does it work? Well, it works for Wanda. She has employed this practice for years.

We all have those mornings when we wake up and, right from the start, know it is going to be a challenging day. You can allow that funk to kick you in the pants all day long and start anew tomorrow, or you can determine that you can change this mood with your own thinking and focus. There are lots of ways to make this happen. A forced smile can turn into a real smile—that is, fake it till you make it—or you can change the negative thoughts in your head to positive ones, whether verbally, mentally, or by writing them down and correcting them on paper. Or perhaps it is time to crawl back into bed, cover up, get up and out on the other side, and try again. The point is you have to do *something* different. Change doesn't happen if you don't change anything.

Journal Prompts

1. What are the benefits of allowing that negative funk to continue? What are the benefits of moving to a perspective of positivity and gratefulness?
2. We all have things that work for us to change our moods. What works for you? Make sure it is a healthy and positive method.
3. What are other methods you would be willing to try?

3

Intentional Growth

JUST DO IT

We've all had those days where we don't want to do anything. I'm actually having one of those days right now. I'm tired for no particular reason, unmotivated, and feel kind of blah. I'm not sick, but my head kind of hurts, but not enough for a Tylenol, and my coffee is just not doing it for me today. I'm still going to work, and I will get through the day, but I'm already thinking about watching some TV tonight and daydreaming about crawling into bed. I have a house that needs to be cleaned, laundry that needs to be folded, a list of errands to run, bills to pay, and of course *work* that needs to be done, but oof … I just seem to be stuck in molasses!

There are lots of things I can do here—drink a little more coffee or double up on the water intake. I could take a power nap (just for transparency, I already tried that, and now I am more tired than before), or I could get up and get going. I have found that this usually works. Sometimes running an errand or taking a short walk seems to get the blood going—and me along with it.

But what about when the sluggishness is emotional and the result of a difficult situation in your life? Depression is a mood disorder and a very real diagnosis; it is also one of the most common mental health issues. There are several different types of depression and, as a result, several different treatments that are recommended. Major depression, bipolar disorder, and other diagnoses received from a medical or mental health provider are *not* what we are discussing today. If you find yourself struggling with the following symptoms all day for more than two weeks, it is important to make an appointment with a specialist. It is amazing what working with a trained professional and making some life changes can do for depression.

Feelings of sadness and//or hopelessness	New or unusual irritability	Loss of interest in things you used to enjoy	Sleep issues—too much, unable to fall asleep, or unable to stay asleep
Lack of energy, even though getting enough sleep	Weight gain or weight loss due to change in food consumption	Anxiety (often a partner with depression)	Fuzzy thinking and/or cognitively sluggish
Feelings of worthlessness	Trouble letting the past go	Cognition issues—struggling to concentrate or make simple decisions	Physical problems with no explanation

**If experiencing a death focus, engaging in self-harm, or thinking of suicide, *do not* wait two weeks, but seek help immediately. There is help and relief available to you. Immediate help is available at 988 or 1-800-273-8255.

Today however, we are talking about situational depression. This is *normal* depression due to something that has occurred in our lives that is difficult. Situational depression is common and can be triggered by life events, such as an important relationship ending, a loved one or pet passing, losing a job or missing out on a promotion, being diagnosed with a significant illness, or receiving other bad news … the list goes on and on. Most of us understand that life is full of ups and downs. Into every life, a little (or a lot of) rain must fall … and sometimes it creates some legitimate feelings of depression. This is a normal reaction to the not so fun stuff of life. This is the kind of depression that usually does not need a specialist or medication—but it sure can benefit from some purposeful action and intentional thinking. Situational depression usually takes care of itself. Time is a great healer, and while you can't rush time, you certainly can decrease the depth of negative emotions you experience. Because situational depression involves mind and body, so do interventions to counteract these unwelcomed feelings. Sometimes you just have to get in there and do what you need to do, even if your motivation is on the floor. The following are some examples:

- *Move.* Walk, run, dance, vacuum, exercise—just do something to get that body moving. Remember Newton's first law of motion: a body at rest will remain at rest unless an outside force acts upon it.
- *Be productive.* Have realistic daily goals that you set for yourself to accomplish—and do them. There is nothing more satisfying than checking things off a list.
- *Protect your environment.* Watch a comedy, listen to uplifting music with a hopeful message (Christian music is a great format for this), read inspirational stories, or engage in some other activity involving feel-good positivity. Avoid dark stuff.
- *Entertain healthy and helpful thoughts.* We can't control what pops into our minds, but we absolutely can control what we focus and ruminate on. If you are already struggling with feelings of depression, you must be hypervigilant for anything that is unneeded and negative. Ditch it—no time for nonproductive thinking.
- *Bible verses.* Speaking of healthy thoughts, Bible verses that remind you of God's purpose, even in the bad stuff, can go a

long way to keep you on the right track. Here are a few of my favorite go-to verses:

- o Romans 8:28: "And we know that in *all things* (emphasis added) God works for the good of those who love Him, who have been called according to His purpose."
- o Matthew 17:20: "He replied, 'Truly I tell you, if you have faith as small as a mustard seed, you can say to this mountain, "Move from here to there," and it will move. Nothing will be impossible for you.'"
- o Joshua 1:9: "Be strong and courageous. Do not be afraid; do not be discouraged, for the Lord your God will be with you *wherever* [emphasis added] you go."

- *Write it out.* This is why there are journal prompts at the end of these devotionals. You can't write as fast as your mind works; therefore, writing helps to slow your brain down and identify thinking errors and untruths that need to be corrected.
- *Get around positive people.* Make sure these folks are good for you and your issues. Avoid those who are going to bring you down and keep you there, even if that means you might have to sit alone with yourself. Believe me when I say there are worse things than being alone.
- *Talk to God.* This may mean praying or just a conversation. He will be there for both!
- *Healthy eating and drinking.* Sometimes this means consuming food and beverages (like water) that you know will be good for you, even if it is not what sounds good.
- *Sleep.* Sometimes rest is the best thing you can do for the mind and body.

None of these suggestions are magic bullets; sometimes you might feel better immediately after engaging in an activity, and sometimes it takes time. The key message here is you must do your part! Just do it and know relief is coming—a mustard seed of faith, my friend.

Journal Prompts

1. What are three things you can do when you need to shake some feelings of depression?
2. What are some things that you should avoid when struggling with feelings of depression?
3. What is going on in your mind right now? Sometimes the best thing to do is just to write—slow that brain down. By the time you are done, your burden will feel lighter.

Intentional Growth

TIME AND PRESSURE
MAKE DIAMONDS

Scientists tell us that it takes between one to three billion years to create a natural diamond. A process of extreme pressure, heat, and time is needed to make the world's most valuable gemstone. But diamonds are not just about looks; they are also the hardest material known to man, capable of high thermal conductivity, and can insulate electrical signals with preciseness. Although the process is difficult and long, the end product has super strengths that make the diamond highly valuable. This is akin to broken bones; when mended, the bone is stronger at the break than the bone around it. This may be hard to imagine because most of us have had something that broke, we glued it back together, only to have it snap easily where it was mended.

One of my favorite pick-me-up songs is Kelly Clarkson's "What Doesn't Kill You Makes You Stronger." You've likely heard this as an old saying too. While this can happen, it is not a guarantee. We can take the rough and tough stuff of life and come out the other side a better, stronger person. Or … we can go the other way. We can become defined by our difficulty, and it becomes a burden we carry. The other dynamic to consider is that you might be in the middle part of the journey, the one to three billion years of time and pressure. Unfortunately, you can't always rush adversity. Ask anyone who has spent time in a gym pumping iron to gain muscle mass. It is not accomplished in an afternoon. It takes time, effort, and commitment; plus, blood, sweat, tears, and pain are involved. Without intentional thoughts and actions, you might not be singing and dancing to Kelly Clarkson's song. Because again, adversity can make you stronger, or it can go the other way.

Jesus was no stranger to adversity. Just because he did everything right and was sinless doesn't mean it was easy—quite the opposite. Hebrews 4:15 says that Jesus understands *every* weakness because he was tempted in *every* way. He gets hurt, loss, and pain—physical and emotional. He didn't just miraculously rise above it all. Although he was all God, he was also all human. He had to work through rough and tough stuff too. So, he gets it; he has been there and done that. Ecclesiastes 1:9 tells us that there is nothing new under the sun. It might be dressed up a bit differently and called a different word—but pain, suffering, and hard times have been around since dirt was a pup. All that time and pressure serve a purpose. Sometimes you can see it, even when you are in the middle of it, and sometimes it seems senseless and pointless. Picking your focus will make all the difference—this I know firsthand.

My first time with cancer, I was all about the purpose. I was confident that cancer would make me a better person, Christian, partner, mother, and friend. The second time around … oof. I was just mad. Instead of looking for the diamonds at the end, I spent a great deal of time feeling sorry for myself and sucking on some sour grapes. James 1:2 says to consider it pure joy to face trials. Well … I was not a good sport the second time around. But the bottom line is that even if you are not feeling what James was saying in his book—which is chuck-full of practical ways to live your life—cognitively and emotionally camping out in a place of purpose in your suffering and focusing on the strength at the end is way more helpful and healthy than the alternative. But you have to do it—think it, meditate on it, and decide this is the path you are going to take, even when you really don't want to because you are not feeling it. Sometimes you have to fake it till you make it and hold on to those promises of what is at the end.

Journal Prompts

1. What are some unhelpful thoughts and ideas that are ruminating in your mind? Once you have a nice list, mark them out with a different color of ink. Don't scribble … just a line. Let this serve as a reminder that you are done with this kind of unhelpful thinking.
2. What are some ideas, Bible verses, or thoughts that are helpful and keep you focused on the end product of your adversity that will result in strength?

5

Intentional Growth

TRUTH—PEOPLE GET TIRED
OF IT AFTER A WHILE

Some of us are just long-standing. This can be a strength, as long-standing people tend to be fiercely loyal, consistent to the end, and finishers. But like any strength, it can also be a weakness. Those of us who are long-standing also have a pertinacity toward pining. Although dysfunctional, I always thought it admirable how Emily Dickenson pined for her lost love and turned her anguish into poetry. I have been known to pine … to wallow … to lick my wounds longer than I should. When you are in the middle of a crisis, you have to take care of business, and you don't have time for pining. But when the crisis has passed and things start to quiet down, this is when it can start.

Here is the problem with pining—lots of people don't get it. Your hard and terrible situation is over; everything is better now. You should be rejoicing, celebrating, and being thankful that you are on the other side of it. But there is the leftover carnage that you have to go through, and it can feel like you go from all kinds of support and help to doing this part all by yourself. And the truth is (and this may hurt a bit), by this time, your loved ones might be tired of your problems. This does not mean they are bad people—by no means! But there are only so many times anyone can watch the same TV show or movie before they get bored with it. Perhaps they feel like it is time for *them* to get some attention and focus.

When you are in the middle of a crisis, it feels like your life slows down, but the world does not. This is where you have a choice. You can pine, and there is nothing wrong with this for a while, or you can shift your attention to giving some love and gratitude to the people who have been helping and supporting you. It may seem ironic, but we are more likely to experience personal growth and insight into the possible purpose of our trials when we focus on others, not ourselves. Second Corinthians 1:4 says, "[God] comforts us in all our troubles, so that we can comfort those in any trouble with the comfort we ourselves receive from God."

The good news is that we have a choice: be intentional or go with what the mind gravitates toward on its own. One choice is going to feel good and productive, and the other is going to be palpable suffering. Do not be disillusioned; pining is a luxury. If you need some time here, allow it for yourself, but at some point, you can't expect others to go there with you. That is when it is time for a paradigm shift—a new focus and some purposeful change in your thinking and behaviors.

Journal Prompts

1. Sometimes you need to pine—go there and hug the suffering no one gets. Write out what is going on in your mind right now, if needed.
2. Who are the people who have been there for you? Write down what they did to support you. Then think about something you could do or say to them to express your gratitude for their support when you needed it the most.

6

Being Thankful and Grateful

PURPOSE IN THE YUCK

If there is something that most optimists and Christians hold on to in times of trouble, it's that there is a reason for everything. Stuff doesn't just happen; there are no coincidences. Sometimes it is evident from the beginning of your difficult circumstance, and sometimes it is not. In those times, you have to look for it and hold on to those promises that God can take anything—*anything*—and turn it for his good. And then there are other times when you have to beg him for insight into how he is going to use this to mold you into a better version of yourself and for his kingdom. That has been my prayer many days, "Please, Lord Jesus, use this for something ... someone ... somehow. Please don't let all this yuck be for nothing."

We know that real and meaningful growth comes in the valleys, not usually on the mountaintops. But what happens when it seems like you have been through more than your share of valleys, and nothing seems to be coming from it? What do you do when it seems like no one really cares, appreciates your struggle, or is even interested in your pain? The first thing ... see what is truly going on: you are sitting on that pity pot, and that is rarely going to be the purpose of a struggle. But getting unstuck from the pity pot can be hard to do, because unsticking yourself is an intentional cognitive and emotional process that only you can make happen.

When it came to my second time with cancer, this time breast cancer at forty-nine, I struggled with many days of "no one cares." When I was twenty-six and had lymphoma, the outpouring of support was humbling. But with breast cancer, I felt very isolated. This was also during COVID-19, and we all had become accustomed to our little bubbles. I had a few people who really showed up, especially at first, but when I was really trying to process everything—in the months after the immediate crisis ended—I felt very alone. It seemed like people just expected me to be okay with everything that had happened. Maybe it was because I was a veteran with this cancer stuff, or because I am pretty good at putting on my poker face and people didn't know how much I was hurting. Maybe it's because I can compartmentalize and stay busy ... and by the time it all finally caught up to me, no one even thought about it. In that time, I felt like it was just me and God ... and as wonderful and amazing as the Lord is, sometimes I felt like I was searching for the purpose in all of this yuck by myself, with little insight.

This is when the intentionality comes in. I had to choose to believe that there is a reason and purpose for the events in my story, even if no one else cared or seemed to notice (oof ... little pity pot sneaking back in there). I had to remind myself that sometimes the reasons will be evident to me in time, or maybe never, but there is a purpose. I also asked for it. Proverbs 4:7 says, "The beginning of wisdom is this: Get wisdom, and whatever you get, get insight" (ESV). God is a provider of wisdom, which brings understanding and insight, but sometimes we have to ask for and seek it. Please, God, open our eyes so we might see the purpose in all this yuck, and give us the courage to do with it what you want.

Journal Prompts

1. Struggling with the pity pot? If so, how?
2. What are some possible purposes that might come from your struggles? How could God use them for you or others?
3. What do you want the purpose to be? How can you take your story and help others?

Being Thankful and Grateful

ALWAYS SOMEONE WORSE

A couple of years after my husband and I were married, we had the opportunity to go to Rome, Italy. It was a short trip, so we stayed primarily in the city. But we took a day trip to Palazzo della Civilta Italiana, a city made of marble, sanctioned by Benito Mussolini during WWII in an attempt to honor himself and woo the 1940 Olympic Games. My husband and I came across a beautiful church with many, many steps, and we sat down to fan ourselves due to the heat and complain about all the walking. Then we watched as a priest in full, long black clergy attire approached the steps and painstakingly struggled to climb each step to the top. We watched in silence as this man summitted; it was a laborious task, and it took a while. We both realized that it was a sacred space we were in with him, and out of reverence, we were quiet. Once the priest made it into the church, my husband turned to me and said, "That is what it means to worship." I understood what he meant. To take on this great physical feat to be in the house of the Lord. In that moment, Alan and I were done complaining about the heat and the walking.

We've all likely had those humbling moments when we're all tied up in our own lives and problems, lamenting about something—very likely a first world problem of some sort—when we see or hear something that makes us stop in our tracks and realize, *I've got* no *problems*. It's important to be thankful and realize that even if you are struggling with something terrible, it could be worse, and there may be someone out there who has it much worse than you.

Even though we may know this, sometimes we need to spend some time in it. With my first cancer, everything happened *very* quickly. My test results were marked "stat," and I got information rapidly. I knew the day after my biopsy that I had cancer, and I started treatment eight days later. I did not experience this kind of treatment the second time around. Test results took several days, even ones that were done in-house. When I asked if the results could be expedited, I was told, in not so many words, that I was not a priority. Really? Cancer is not a priority? The fact that I was a cancer survivor didn't seem to matter. In an attempt to try to keep my sanity while I waited, I made lists of things to be grateful for, even if it turned out to be bad news. This exercise helped me to focus on God being in control. The idea that even though I might be in for a not so fun ride, I was likely going to be okay. Just for today, I was alive and healthy. God had blessed me over and over again, and he had provided for me so far; I could rest in the confidence that he was not going to stop providing now. It helped. It didn't make my anxiety magically go away or make me feel on-top-of-the-world happy, but it did get my mind in a better place with a healthier focus.

Journal Prompts

1. Make a list of things for which you can be thankful. This is the only prompt for today, to allow you to come up with as many items as you have time to list. Once you start, you will likely find that the ideas really start rolling. Nothing is too big or too small for this list.

8

Being Thankful and Grateful

DIFFERENCE BETWEEN BEING THANKFUL AND GRATEFUL

Thankful and *grateful* are terms that are often used at the same time and interchangeably … but are they really the same? Turns out there are some crucial differences in these kissing cousin terms. *Thankful is* the simpler of the two terms. In order to be thankful, something has to happen that benefits us. You receive an unexpected compliment or gift from a friend, someone opens a door for you, or someone goes out of their way to do you a favor. It's a reaction to something from which we have profited. As children, we are taught to say *thank you* when someone does something nice for us.

Being grateful is more complicated. This is an intentional attitude and cognitive approach. Being grateful involves being thankful, then takes it a step further. It means to look for things to be thankful for, even things that may not benefit us in a profitable manner. One of the keys to living in recovery for those who struggle with substance-use disorder is living a life of gratitude. As a social worker, I spent nineteen years working with clients struggling with substance-use disorders. Alcoholics Anonymous (AA) is not kidding when they say that addiction is cunning, baffling, and powerful. Spend enough time in recovery circles, and you are going to meet some of the most amazing people who have survived unimaginable things. Talk about a group of people who have spent all nine of their lives! You will also meet *old-timers*, which is a term reserved for those who have been able to live a considerable time of consistent sobriety. Because of their recovery, old-timers have a common characteristic—brutal honesty, which I enjoy. When you are friends with an old-timer, you never have to worry if they are telling you the truth or if they are just being nice—they shoot straight with you. The other commonality they have is an attitude of gratitude for the things that have happened in their lives—including their addiction, the events that occurred when they were in their disease process, and, most importantly, their recovery.

I have heard old-timers talk about how grateful they are for their alcoholism and addictions, because it helps them to appreciate today and the fact that they don't have to live that life anymore. It sounds backward to be grateful for hard times and difficult situations, but these are the things that have the potential to make us better. The apostle Paul knew this. He is certainly qualified as someone who adopted an attitude of gratitude. In 2 Corinthians 12:9–10, he writes,

> My grace is sufficient for you, for my power is made perfect in weakness. Therefore I will boast all the more gladly about my weakness, so that Christ's power may rest on me. That is why, for Christ's sake, I delight in weakness, in insults, in hardships, in persecutions, in difficulties. For when I am weak, I am strong.

Great couple of verses. These are common verses that are highlighted in Bibles, memorized, used as inspirational decorations, or even tattooed on bodies. Yep—they are that good! But here is something to consider. Verse 8—the verse right before it—reads, "Three times I pleaded with the Lord to take it away from me." What does that mean? Maybe Paul didn't *always* delight in hardships. I am certain there were times when Paul was fed up with all the difficulties he encountered, and while he was doing the work of the Lord no less. I imagine there were conversations between Paul and God that went something like this: "Lord, I am breaking my neck out here trying to love these horrible people to you. Could I just get some help with the whole persecution stuff? Seriously, God, I don't mean to sound like a future Janet Jackson here, but what have you done for me lately?"

There is a reason Paul purposefully and intentionally chose to be grateful for all these things, even when God did not remove or stop the difficulties he was experiencing. Choosing to be grateful puts your mind in a much better place. A place where you can see the blessings and promises of provision. It also trickles down into more positive emotional and biological health. It puts you in a place to make better decisions and to behave in a more productive manner. This is why old-timers live a life of gratitude and strongly recommend it for those who are trying to string together long-term sobriety. It works—not magically, not easily, and certainly not intuitively. It is a choice. Not one I have always made myself, but boy does it make a difference when I do. Additionally, it is a constant battle. We must continue to choose to be grateful.

Journal Prompts

1. Are you choosing to be grateful today? If not, why not? If yes, how it that working for you?
2. Just for today, what is one difficult thing that you can be grateful for? What are some lessons you have learned?

9

Being Thankful and Grateful

TIMING IS EVERYTHING

As a proud momma of two beautiful, smart, and gifted children, I have been known to wear mom goggles. I like to think that I have it together a bit more than Beverly Goldberg (if you have not seen *The Goldbergs*, stream now!), but in truth, I'm right there with her. Our son is brilliant—truly. I can't believe I produced a child with his brain. Math and science are like a second language to this child. From kindergarten through twelfth grade, he never made less than an A on a report card. He graduated top of his class and scored a 35 on his ACT, all while being involved in sports, band, church youth group, drama, and working part-time. Amazing, right? So when he was passed over for a full-ride fellowship that he was perfect for, it took me to my knees (literally in the kitchen of our home). He was in the final group, he had a great interview, his application and supporting evidence were unmatched, and as we walked around the campus that day, I just *knew* he had it in the bag. I thought God had ordained it. But then, two weeks later, the letter came that said he was not selected. Our whole family was hurt by the news but no one more than my son. He and I talked of it often during his first two years of college. Despite being turned down for the full-ride fellowship, Noah still chose to attend the college, and sometimes he had some salty moments about not receiving the honor.

During Noah's second year of college, after changing his major and having great anxiety over his lack of knowing what he wanted to do in the future, he had a revelation. Thank goodness he didn't get the full-ride fellowship. As a fellow, you are paired with a professor in your major, and for the duration of your time at the university, you engage in research with this professor. By his second year of college, Noah detested the major he initially declared. What a burden to be saddled with—to have to continue to research with a professor in a subject matter he could no longer stand to maintain his scholarship. Think of the time and work he would be required to sacrifice, not to mention the mental anguish. The lack of a fellowship meant he had total and complete freedom to explore at will across multiple academic fields.

We've all had those moments—those blessings in disguise—when we're disappointed by how things turned out, only to realize later that it was the best thing that could have happened. Usually in those moments, or maybe later in a time of reflection, we come to realize that there is purpose in the disappointment. Perhaps it's because something bigger and better is around the corner, or maybe we just aren't ready for what we want yet. We need more time to grow, mature, develop a skill, or acquire knowledge. And sometimes … maybe God just wants us to be uncomfortable and to simply sit in it and trust what he is doing. In our disappointment and struggles, we need to hang on to those promises. God's timing is perfect, yet rarely does it match up with our plans and timetable. God is like an expert chess player in the sky, and sometimes we just have to wait for his strategic move.

The day Noah had his revelation, he was still struggling with what God's plan was for his future and when he would receive the guidance and direction he was seeking. Noah had been praying about his future and where God wanted him for several years but felt like he was getting no answers. As his mother, I had total and complete confidence that God had knitted together this amazing young man—with his specific strengths, skills, talents, personality, temperament, and challenges— for a specific purpose. I can pray Jeremiah 29:11–12 over my son, but sometimes, for whatever reason, God makes us wait. No one likes it, but in the waiting, we can find unexpected growth, faith, encouragement, and peace. But like most everything else, you are going to have to be intentional in the waiting.

Journal Prompts

1. What are some blessings in disguise you have experienced in the past?
2. What might be some reasons or purposes for your season of waiting?
3. We know that our God will never fail, so what kind of promises and/or past experiences of provision can you hold on to now?

Being Thankful and Grateful

MAKE YOUR MESS YOUR MESSAGE

"Make your mess your message." Isn't that a great life philosophy? I would love to take credit for that catchy and meaningful statement, but it's not mine. The phrase was coined by Robin Roberts, a TV broadcaster who has taken on a number of challenges in her life. She is a proud woman of color, as well as one of the first open members of the LGBTQ+ community to be a news journalist. Additionally, she was one of the first female ESPN sportscasters and paved the way for others who identify as female to banter about sports stats and game strategy with the OGs and show the world that girls can talk sports too. She is also a strong woman of faith who uses her faith and dependency on God to deal with difficult life situations. So far in her journey, Ms. Roberts has survived cancer twice: breast cancer in 2007, involving surgery, chemo, and radiation; and myelodysplastic syndrome in 2012, a form of cancer involving bone marrow cells, which involved a bone marrow transplant. No cancer is fun, but having a bone marrow transplant involves an arduous journey of physical and emotional depletion. However, Ms. Roberts was able to come through her affliction stronger, wiser, and more grateful than ever, even authoring a book titled *Everybody's Got Something*.

I am no Robin Roberts. I'm still struggling, and my journey is not nearly as difficult or death defying. Writing this book became my own personal support group because when I really needed one, they had all been canceled due to the COVID-19 pandemic. But what I discovered is that I knew what I needed to do to be more successful with the aftermath of a trauma or crisis. Focusing on being thankful and grateful is where recovery is. It is purposeful, intentional … a choice, and one you must choose daily. Some days, this choice comes easily, but on other days, I actively reject it. The idea of making your mess your message means being open about your struggles. While Ms. Roberts is an example of how to deal with adversity in a positive way, I am confident she had her own struggles and moments of not following her own advice. But there is just something healing and freeing about being honest with your plight. It helps you to eventually get to the point that you are ready to do what you can to change your struggle and choose to focus on the things that are going to benefit you—like being thankful and grateful.

Journal Prompts

1. Make a list of things that you can be thankful and grateful for in your journey. If you have already done this, see what new items you can add to the list.
2. Why is being intentional about your focus important?
3. When you are not feeling like being thankful and grateful, what can you tell yourself as a reminder?

11

Joy

DON'T MISS THE GOOD STUFF

I was twenty-six when I was diagnosed with Hodgkin lymphoma, and it has continued to be a defining part of my life since that phone call on October 15, 1996. At the time, I was single (although dating my now husband), hours away from family, and had just started a new job. But from the moment of diagnosis, I had a wicked peace. *Wicked* being defined in the scientific sense of something that cannot be defined, explained, or rationalized. You, as the reader, may already know where I am heading with this. What I was experiencing was that peace that passes all understanding, which, thankfully, God provides liberally (Philippians 4:7). There were times in my apartment when it was just me, God, and whatever scary issues I was contemplating about my cancer, finances, or future, and I felt like God was right there with me. In my mind, I envisioned myself sitting in God's lap, like I used to sit in my daddy's lap as a child, with the sense of utter protection. Those were good times—very special moments of tangible experiences with my heavenly Father.

It didn't take long for me to realize that chemo was no fun, and I was in for a marathon, not a sprint, of traveling through the wilderness. This journey had the potential to make me a better social worker, colleague, daughter, sister, future wife, mother, and all-around person. It was all in how I approached it. Posttraumatic growth is intentional and uses purposeful skills to deal more effectively with adversity and challenges.

Anything aversive or frightening, or any event that significantly changes our world has the potential to be traumatic—or at the least upsetting. But that doesn't mean that we can't glean from it positive and life-affirming lessons and dependence on God. While I would never voluntarily sign up for cancer, it's not all bad; it's all in how you spin it. When struggling with significant life events, you may not have control over what is happening, but you do have control over your perspective. Joy is a choice, not a feeling, and one we have to make daily. It's just that some days, choosing joy is much harder than others.

Journal Prompts

1. How have you seen/felt God in your situation?
2. What are some potential benefits of your situation?
3. What is one slice of joy you can remind yourself of when you are struggling?

12

Joy

THERE IS SOMETHING TO
BE LEARNED HERE

I had a number of wonderful teachers in my life … some stinky ones too. One teacher who made an impression on me was my senior-year English teacher. I wasn't anything special to her. I was an average student with atrocious spelling, and I went to high school before papers were written with computers. Therefore, my English papers were either handwritten (which was not pretty) or completed on a typewriter. Either way, the document was full of mistakes. This is just how I roll! Regardless, one of the pieces of life advice I remember my English teacher giving us was that boredom is your own responsibility. No matter where you are, there is always something to be learned, observed, reviewed, or contemplated. If you are complaining about being bored, you are missing opportunities.

Trauma and negative life events can be like that. Now, if you are reading this, and this is not landing well, it may be that your event is too fresh or raw for this line of thinking. Understandable. Hopefully, in time, you will get there. For now, it's probably best to pick a different devotion and come back to this one later. But for those of you who are intrigued, there is work to be done. What are some things that I have learned through two battles with cancer? Here are just a few:

- The Lord will provide. Maybe not exactly the way I would have liked it or as quickly as I hoped for, but he always comes through.
- People you hardly know will support you and pray for you during tough times, and it is very humbling.
- People you thought would be there for you in tough times don't show up, and it is disappointing.
- If you need something, ask for it, because no one can read your mind.
- Cancer has a way of realigning your priorities, which is life affirming.
- Once you are healthy and the crisis has passed, your priorities get out of whack at a surprisingly fast rate.
- All emotions were given to us for a reason, and you are going to feel what you feel—whether you like it or not, whether it is embarrassing, shameful, or inspirational.
- Getting through a negative life event is not a contest, but if you feel like it is, it is because you are the one keeping score.
- Just because you did cancer well the first time around don't mean jack for the second.

So—this last bullet point. If I were giving myself a grade for how I did cancer, I would give myself a B+ for my first time. I came through the experience with a number of positive learned lessons. But the second time around, oof, more like a C or C-. Why the difference? There are lots of possibilities that come to mind. I was older, I knew more about what I was going to have to go through, I had a husband and children I was going to have to drag through the muck with me, and I was busy. But the real reason is I didn't turn to the Lord like I had when I was twenty-six. Was it because at forty-nine I thought I could handle it on my own? No … it was because instead of turning to the Lord, crawling into his Word, looking for things to be thankful for, and seeing this as an opportunity for growth, I had a bad attitude and was mad. There is really no other way to say it. I was dismayed that I had to do this again. It really is amazing how quickly my attitude took over the way I was processing and dealing with my crisis. Add in some hurtful behaviors and statements from some unhealthy people, and my attitude was going downhill and picking up speed.

To make matters worse, I was embarrassed by my anger and my bad attitude. Therefore, I did the worst thing I could do—I hid it from everyone. I put on a brave face, said the right things, and allowed unhelpful thinking errors to set up in my mind. I knew logically this was not a good idea and that this would all come back to roost at some point, but mental survival makes for a strange cognitive bedfellow. The first time I had cancer, I kept a journal. Almost daily I would write in it, and I would be encouraged by what God was doing in my life through this difficult time. Second time around, I was determined *not* to journal but ended up caving because it was the only way I could process all the yuck and anger in my head. But this journal was *not* encouraging. It was full of ugliness about the injustices I was experiencing. There was not much God in it at all. How did it turn out? Well, after months of going down this lonely and unfulfilling path, I decided that perhaps I needed to listen to my senior high school English teacher and be determined to learn from this event. What I was doing was technically working, and I was getting through the breast cancer stuff, but I was not doing it well. Not much positive growth was coming from it, just more yuck, anger, stinking thinking, and pity pot material. Thankfully, I had the presence of mind to know that I did not want to get stuck here. I knew that the longer I hung out in this unhealthy place, the more likely I was to remain for far longer than I intended.

So did I turn on a dime and fix myself right up with a heartfelt prayer to God and asking for his forgiveness for my bad attitude? No … it wasn't that simple for me. But what I did do was start to be purposeful in how I was looking at things. For sure, I was dealt some unfun stuff, but it was up to me to decide to learn something from all of this. It was an opportunity to grow—to move my C/C- up the grade scale. And maybe, just maybe, use this journey to help someone else grow too.

Journal Prompts

1. What is not working for you as you approach your negative life events?
2. What could you do differently that would make things more positive?
3. What is stopping you from making that change?

13

FORGIVENESS ... I KNOW,
BUT IT'S IMPORTANT

Out of all of these chapters, this one might be the hardest for me to write. We all have those paradoxical parts of ourselves. I pride myself on being nonjudgmental, and I can see the good in lots of people and situations where others cannot. However, if someone hurts me emotionally and does so purposefully, I can hold on to that for a long time ... a *long time.* Even worse, most of the time, the other person has no idea they have hurt me because I am also anticonflict; I just stuff it away and try to deal with it myself. One thing you learn about those who struggle with substance-use disorder is that resentment is a huge relapse trigger. It does not make logical sense, but in the mind of someone who struggles with addiction, picking up and using their drug of choice feels like a justifiable way to get back at someone who has wronged them. The thought process is, *I'm mad at you, so I am going to use ... and that will show 'em!* Again ... this does not make any logical sense to me, but to someone who is struggling with addiction and resentment, it makes perfect sense.

When it comes to me, however, I will be unforgiving to someone, and it seems completely justified, even though it is taking up considerable mental energy, keeps me in a negative mindset, and robs me of the freedom and peace that comes with forgiveness. I will reject forgiving someone even in the face of all the grace and forgiveness that has been afforded me by Christ. The egotism! Forgiveness is a gift you give yourself; for the other person, well … that's just gravy. It is like unburdening yourself. So *why* do I struggle with this? I know that holding on to personal grudges is pointless, hurtful to my walk with Christ and others, and sinful. It also spills over. You think you can keep all that negativity to yourself, but in time, it comes out in how you treat loved ones, coworkers, and friends. It affects the way you look at the world. It's like a bad spot in a container of strawberries—no matter how pretty, delicious, and nutritious they are, if you don't get that moldy one out, it is going to ruin the whole lot! When you hold on to all that yuck and don't forgive, you create a prison and a poison for yourself mentally.

So here is the really important part of this reading … how do you forgive the unforgivable? It's something you just do. It's a process. It's a daily thing, and some days you do better than others. Acknowledge what you should do, take responsibility for any of your part in the conflict, pray about it and pray for the offender, rinse and repeat. Eventually, the resentment melts and the bitterness decreases, and wisdom emerges to see the benefits of letting all the yuck go. Or at least that is what I'm hoping for! In twelve-step programs, a common recommendation for resentment is to say a prayer of goodness every day for twenty-one days for the person you are struggling to forgive. I have tried this before, and I do well for a few days, and then I forget, and next time I have a bad forgiveness day, I am right back to day one again. Other times, I have made it all twenty-one days, and it makes a significant difference. I don't know how or why; I just know that it works. Maybe the magic comes from the intentional focus changing my perspective. I don't know how God does it, forgives and forgets in an instant. Psalm 103:12 says, "As far as the east is from the west, so far has he removed our transgressions from us." Thank goodness God doesn't look at us like we look at one another and need twenty-one days minimum to forgive!

Journal Prompts

1. What are the wrongs you are struggling to let go?
2. Write a prayer for someone who has hurt you. A prayer of blessing over their lives. You guessed it—now you get to pray this prayer for twenty-one days over this person.

14

Joy

SOMETIMES YOU BRING IT—SOMETIMES YOU NEED IT (SUPPORT GROUPS)

There are movies that are so good that when you're thumbing through TV stations and you come across it, you'll watch some of it. Doesn't matter what part you come in on; there are so many meaningful scenes that a little goes a long way. One of those movies for me is *Fried Green Tomatoes* (1991), a story about friendship, secrets, and ladies taking care of business when no one else could. If you have not seen the movie, I highly recommend it, and the book is even better because it comes with recipes at the end.

I sometimes show a clip of the movie in class when we discuss the importance of friendship, especially close friends, and the benefits that come from having at least one trusted "shovel friend." A shovel friend is someone who will show up with shovels, help you bury whatever needs to be (figuratively or logistically), ask no questions, and never tell another living soul. In a pivotal part of *Fried Green Tomatoes*, long after the two main characters, Idgie and Ruth, had a monumental falling out, Ruth sends word that she needs help to deal with her domestically abusive husband. Idgie shows up and brings Ruth to live with the Threadgoode family. No "I told you he was bad news" or "I tried to tell you girl, but you wouldn't listen," and certainly not an "I knew it all along—that someday I would be cleaning up your mess of a life." No. All she gives is precious, soul-healing acceptance and support.

Support groups can do this. You have to find the right one, but when you do, you can walk in and immediately feel acceptance, understanding, and support from people who *get it*. Sounds wonderful, right? The problem is that lots of people out there have hang-ups about support groups. And let me tell you, the people who trash support groups the harshest are usually the ones who need them the most. As someone who has worked in recovery circles for more than two decades, there really is no substitute for the support and accountability of a twelve-step group. I have heard many excuses and objections for why people won't even give a support group a try. Usually something like "How is sitting around listening to other people's problems going to help me?" Well, let me list just some of the ways:

- First off, sitting around telling sob stories about one's life is *not* what support groups do. Support groups are about positive change and growth.
- There is a central message of hope to support groups, even when situations seem hopeless.
- Support groups are centered around a specific issue or need, so everyone speaks the same language.
- These are organized meetings with start and end times, usually sixty to ninety minutes; this is not an open mic event that goes on for hours.
- Support group meetings have rotating subjects that systematically address the different challenging aspects of the central issue.
- Support groups stick with you when you are ugly acting and not very nice to be around, when you are making progress on your issues, when you get stuck, and when you regress.
- When no one else in your world understands, someone in that room will.
- They catch you in your stinking, unhelpful, and error-filled thinking, and they call it out.
- You feel encouraged and renewed when you leave.
- There are people in the group who are farther down this road, and they will partner with you one on one and help show you the way.
- There is usually coffee ... and sometimes snacks!

If you are struggling and you are rejecting the idea of a support group, I would highly recommend you try going. But there are other things you need to do too, like keep an open mind, drop the negative attitude, and try the group more than just one time. Additionally, if there are multiple groups for your issue, try different ones to see which feels like home. Only then can you reject the notion of support groups.

I would have given anything to have had a support group of women who had been through breast cancer. However, I had breast cancer during COVID-19, and all the face-to-face groups in my area had been suspended indefinitely. I tried to get into an online group but was rejected because they had to limit their number and my presentation was not deemed worthy enough—that was a nice emotional sucker punch. There is just something healing and meaningful in being able to share with others who get it and will not pass judgment. It is also reassuring to know that the things you think, feel, and experience are not unique but common to the plight. If there is a support group out there for you and you are being resistive, get over yourself and show up! Be intentional. And if a trusted loved one has recommended you try a support group because of your mood, attitude, behaviors, and/or general approach, then you *really* need to give it a try. And it doesn't matter if you are in the middle of a challenging time or it was twenty years ago. If you've got unresolved issues, you've got unresolved issues! It is like when someone offers you a breath mint; they aren't just being nice … they are trying to tell you something. To reject a support group is a wasted opportunity for hope, strength, and healing.

Journal Prompts

1. What are the potential support groups in your area or online? Remember that Celebrate Recovery at area churches will work for any hurt, hang-up, or habit, and all are welcome—not just church members.
2. What kind of support would you like to have from a support group?
3. What is holding you back from going?

15

Joy

WANT TO KEEP THEM GUESSING?
REJOICE IN YOUR CRISIS

I grew up in church, and we did not have children's church, which meant that I went to service with my parents after I was too old to be in the nursery. I learned a number of lessons in "big church" as a child, like how to fill in all the empty spaces in the letters of the bulletin, how to play tic-tac-toe with myself, how to count items in the sanctuary, and how to sit still and be quiet. Sometimes in those still and quiet moments, I would actually catch something that the pastor said.

One Sunday, a pastor by the name of Dr. Bernard Holmes came to preach due to the absence of our regular pastor. Ironically, he would later be one of my professors at Southwest Baptist University (best school ever!). Dr. Holmes was especially unique in that he was originally from New Zealand, and he had the most beautiful accent. I'm not sure what the title or topic of his message was that Sunday, but I remember him saying, "Brothers and sisters, we must rejoice in all things—even the hard things. I just lost my job, praise the Lord. I lost my house in a fire, praise the Lord. I've been diagnosed with cancer, praise the Lord." That last one is the one that got me to stop daydreaming and pay closer attention. *Praise the Lord for cancer? That can't be right.* As a child who grew up watching her younger brother survive leukemia, I could not even start to understand this statement.

I mentioned this at lunch after church, and both my parents were in full agreement. Yes, praise the Lord for cancer, because he will provide. You have an opportunity to experience God in the valley, and although it is scary and no one *wants* to go through challenging times, there is no deeper experience with your heavenly Father than when you are in the middle of it. Not to mention it's so much better than wallowing in it.

Optimism and positivity are mindsets that we choose … as is joy. Biblical joy is looking at difficult circumstances and suffering as opportunities to grow closer to God and develop as a Jesus-loving person. Somedays, we're all over this idea—proclaiming to the world that we will rejoice in the good and the bad. We might even recite James 1:2–3 by heart, "Consider it pure joy, my brothers and sisters, whenever you face trials of many kinds, because you know that the testing of your faith produces perseverance." And other days, we might not be feeling the joy that comes from our world falling down around us. But here's the bottom line—we can. We can choose joy. We can decide that there is a reason for all the madness that we are going through, and we can decide that we are going to claim this, because the alternative is nonproductive and unhelpful. Be cautious because there are some sneaky joy stealers out there. They include things like pride, social comparison, selfishness, anxiety, resentment, unforgiveness, complaining, repressing anger, spending time with negative people, and expecting perfection from yourself.

Joy is more than a feeling; it's a state of mind, and you may have days where you are in a constant battle with your mind. Like so many things in life, joy is a journey, not so much a destination, and there are going to be lumps and bumps along the way. Give yourself permission to incorporate imperfect progress rather than absolute perfection in your journey. Like Dory says in *Finding Nemo*, "When life gets you down, you know what you gotta do? … Just keep swimming, just keep swimming, just keep swimming." Joy is biblical, it is obedient, and it is strategic. It gets us farther down the road with more internal resources and a little less damaged. It is a win-win, with the extra bonus of shocking and surprising those around you. And they will ask, "How are you doing so well with _____ in your life right now?" You will have the perfect answer. "Because I choose joy, or at least for this moment."

Journal Prompts

1. In your own words, what is joy?
2. Are there any cognitive thoughts that are stealing your joy? If so, write them down, draw a line through them, and create a new thought that reflects joy.
3. Are you purposefully not choosing joy? That is okay. We all have moments, days, or even weeks like that. Why do you think you are stuck here?

16

Acceptance

EVERYTHING IS NORMAL BECAUSE EVERYTHING IS ABNORMAL

We like to tell people how to feel, especially when it comes to topics with which we have experience. And while people are often well intentioned in their directives, they are not thinking of you. That may sound harsh, but it's a life truth. When people tell you how you should feel, what they are really telling you is how they think they would feel if they were in the situation. If the person has been through the situation themselves, they are even more confident in how you should feel. But here is the rub—they are *not* you. No one has your personality, temperament, individual experiences, worldview, values, or dozens of other factors that make you the individual and unique person you are. Therefore, whatever you are feeling about your situation is normal (with very few exceptions—we'll talk more about this later), because difficult events are abnormal, and they create whatever feelings they create.

It might be helpful to talk about what these two terms, *normal* and *abnormal*, mean. Common synonyms for *normal* are typical, standard, and common. Basically, your run-of-the-mill ordinary stuff. Difficulty, adversity, and trauma—*not* normal. *Abnormal*, on the other hand, is a deviation from the customary that is undesirable and troublesome. This is the category where difficulties, adversity, and trauma belong, and when you find yourself in abnormal territory, well, all bets are off when it comes to emotions.

The Lord created humans with an array of complex emotions. What's more, we can experience multiple emotions at the same time. Sometimes these emotions go together, like anxiety and fear. Other times, the combination can be polar opposites like sadness and happiness—the very definition of bittersweet. Even more perplexing is the life span of emotions. They bubble up; then they dissipate. Sometimes they are short-lived, and other times they stick around for a while. But one particularly important thing to remember about feelings is that they are not an accurate source of information concerning what is really going on. Feelings are commonly exaggerated, based on inaccurate information, or distorted for other reasons. This is why it's really important not to make decisions on emotions, because the decision you made at the time that felt so right and justified may look very different once those feelings have passed.

Here is the good news about emotions—you have some control. Emotions are strongly influenced by your cognitive thoughts. Therefore, if you are struggling with emotions that are troubling to you or creating problems, you can take strategic steps to intentionally think about your situation in a different and more helpful way. It takes time for cognition to trickle down to emotions. Just thinking happy thoughts is not going to fix emotional issues completely, but it certainly can help. Additionally, God can handle your emotions, no matter how unsightly they might be, and he is the only one who really understands what you are going through.

Oh, remember earlier when I said we would talk about the rare exceptions to normal emotions? People deal with difficulties in vastly different ways. Sometimes the emotions make sense, and sometimes they seem quite odd. This certainly is one of the reasons social workers believe that *normal* is simply a setting on your dryer. However, there are two emotions/reactions that are not normal and need to be addressed immediately: suicidal thoughts with intention and/or violence toward self or others. If you find yourself here, please call 988 or 1-800-273-8255 for free, confidential support.

Journal Prompts

1. What are some emotions your situation has stirred up for you?
2. What emotions would you like to change?
3. What are some thoughts that you can identify that might be feeding the emotions you dislike, and what are some different thoughts you should focus on to change unwanted emotions?

17

Acceptance

PART OF MY STORY

One of my most favorite war movies is *The Great Escape*. The movie was released in 1963 and is based on the true story of a group of British soldiers who methodically planned and executed a daring escape from a WWII German POW camp. Although the true events that inspired the movie did not involve any Americans, Hollywood decided to bring in Steve McQueen and James Garner (who is *so* good-looking!) into the film, which takes away from some of its historical accuracy. Still, the movie was nominated and won several awards. If you have not seen it, I highly recommend it—especially if you are a WWII buff.

Now, while I love this movie and will sit down and watch parts of it if I happen to see it while scrolling through the channels, I will only watch it to a certain part. I don't mean to spoil the ending for anyone, but it is mostly sad, with only a couple of successful escapes. Therefore, I don't watch that part. I watch until they all get out of the tunnel and escape into the woods … and then I turn it off. In my magical world, they all make it out of Nazi Germany and back home to their loved ones. I do this with other movies too. In *Shawshank Redemption*, I never watch when Brooks kills himself. In my version, Brooks meets a lovely older woman who has lost her sight and needs someone to read to her. She hires Brooks, the two fall in love, and they take care of each other for the rest of their days. Oh, if only our lives could be so easily manipulated. If there is a part of your life that you don't like, you could just not watch it, redo the scenes you don't care for, or make up your own alternative ending. But we all know that's not how it works.

God has a mighty plan for everyone. Ephesians 2:10 reminds us, "For we are God's handiwork, created in Christ Jesus to do good works, which God prepared in advance for us to do." None of us are mistakes; we were all intentionally given spiritual gifts, and we all serve a purpose. Additionally, God's will is always better than any life plan we could produce for ourselves. And while I logically know these things, sometimes I don't always feel it or believe them. Sometimes I am flat-out unhappy about it. I don't want my purpose in life to be someone who talks about how she dealt with cancer … twice. And heaven forbid, please don't add any episodes in the future for additional sharable fodder—I have had quiet enough, thank you! I have already shared with you some of my movie-watching idiosyncrasies, but there are more. I also don't watch movies or TV shows where the main focus is cancer. I don't do survivor walks either … they mess with my head too much. I find that living with a certain level of avoidance works well for me. But in truth, it's not particularly effective. I likely think about cancer more than most people. I have since I was a small child witnessing my younger brother survive childhood leukemia.

I try to be grateful for God's provision in my life—even things that confuse me. I work to remind myself that there is a plan in place and a reason these things are (or are not) happening. And like lots of people, there have been events in my life that made no sense to me while they were occurring, but in time, I was able to look back and see God's mighty hand at work and be grateful for his masterful chess-playing, four-moves-ahead-of-you actions. But there are other *gifts* from God or events in my life for which I am not always grateful. I try to take solace in the idea that all these things come together to make me the person I am today—warts and all. The trick is to just accept what you've got and make the most of it. Easy to say, extremely hard to do sometimes.

So how is it we can be grateful for the bad and terrible stuff? The Bible tells us that the only way we can really grow in our faith is to deal with adversity. Romans is all about the rewards of suffering. It's when the chips are down that you discover who you can really count on—and let's face it, humans are *not* it. People are flawed. Individuals will eventually let you down. Even the ones who really love you make mistakes, don't come through, and disappoint. The Lord is omnipotent (all-powerful), omniscient (all-knowing), and omnipresent (always present), and I have struggled with feeling like he let me down. Don't worry—God can handle me talking this way; I won't get struck by lightning. God can take our anger, disappointment, questioning, doubt, and displeasure. If he couldn't, he would not have given us all these emotions—the fun positive ones, and the not-so-fun negative ones. And unlike the movies, sometimes we can't avoid them, turn them off, or fast-forward through the bad parts. We simply have to go through it and all the muck that goes with it. If we are sticking with the movie motif, think of it this way. What is a movie without some suspense, scary moments, and plot twists? Nothing special. So perhaps, if nothing else, we can be thankful and grateful for a nonboring existence … and then maybe we can start to add a few more things to that list of being grateful. You might be amazed at what we can be grateful for once the thankful juices start flowing.

Journal Prompts

1. What are some events in your life that you are struggling to be grateful for?
2. Looking at these events, what are some lessons learned that could lead to feelings of gratitude? Dig deep.
3. What might be a future plan with this event? How might God use this time of negativity for his good … and/or yours?

18

Acceptance

BUFFERING AND LOADING

All of us have likely had the wonderful experience of waiting for a computer to do its thing. The spinning wheel that tells you something is happening … but it might take a while. And the longer the spinning goes, you know, the more likely it is there is some kind of problem that is going to require trying again, a restart of the computer, or a dead end. There are all kinds of computer terms out there, but two similar ones are *buffering* and *loading*. Buffering is when a computer is loading information into a system so it can perform its duty, and loading is setting a platform in place so the system can work. In order for a computer to work with most systems, loading has to be totally complete. However, computers can start working while buffering but can only go so far. You wait for a while, and you can go a little further, and then you might have to wait again. Anyone who has attempted to watch a video on a computer or phone has likely experienced buffering. The video will start, and you get to watch a bit of it, then it pauses, plays a bit more, and then pauses again. This is buffering, and depending on how badly you want to see something, you might put up with the ten seconds of video to one minute of buffering, or you might just give up, call it quits, and try again later.

Acceptance can be a lot like buffering and loading. There are times that we have to know or experience the whole event/situation before acceptance is possible, and there are other times when we buffer—we deal with small chunks of a difficult situation, and we have the mental fortitude or spiritual faith to accept what is happening and keep moving. Some people seem to have blind faith and acceptance for any and all of life's events. I am not such a person. It takes me a minute ... or several minutes (and by this, I mean the *Urban Dictionary* definition of a *minute*: a significant amount of time—weeks, months, or years). I've always been a slow learner and someone who seems to have to make more than just one mistake to learn her lesson. It also just depends. With my first go-around with cancer, I accepted my diagnosis and what was happening pretty quickly without much fuss. But my second time around ... well, there was far more buffering involved. The kind of buffering that gets bogged down and makes you want to just throw your phone/computer out of frustration.

Acceptance is all about perspective and attitude. We have all been in a situation where we had a good and positive attitude, which made dealing with life's frustrations easier. Likewise, we have all had an unproductive and negative attitude, which made us an ugly sight to be seen—to ourselves and anyone else who crossed our paths. What makes the difference? All kinds of things—how well rested we are, if and what we have eaten, what other life events are going on, general mental health, and countless other factors. In recovery circles, they use the acronym HALT—don't get too hungry, angry, lonely, or tired because we are more likely to make poor decisions when we are in one or more of these categories. Therefore, if you find yourself in a situation, and you would like to just jump forward to the acceptance part, there are things you can do to speed up the process: take a nap, eat a meal, and protect your emotional environment, and so on. Though, for full disclosure, rarely can you just magically accept something aversive. Even if you do, watch out; time has a way of bringing it back around for a reckoning.

If we want to work on acceptance, what we are really working on is our perspective of the event. And when we are dealing with a negative event that has invaded our world and thrown everything out of whack, a negative perspective is par for the course. When it comes to purposefully and intentionally changing your perspective of an event from negative to positive ... or at least not quite so negative, the fastest and more effective way is to get grateful. I just heard that internal groan. *Here we go again with the being grateful.* But the simple bottom line is being grateful is how you get your mind where it needs to be so the feelings can start to follow suit. That is how it works; your thoughts (perspective) are directly related to your feelings (acceptance/nonacceptance), and your feelings lead to your behaviors (displays of nasty/positive attitude). Purposefully changing your perspective through being grateful can feel a lot like math homework when you were in grade school. No one liked doing thirty problems of long division, but you do it because that is what you do. You may not feel like being grateful, but you force yourself, because this is what you do to ultimately get to where you want to be. Now, you don't *have* to. You can stay in a negative attitude and list all the reasons why you are struggling. Much like not doing your math homework, you can either do it at home and turn it in on time, or you can stay in during recess and do it … but eventually, you will come to the conclusion that you might as well just do the homework already and move on without the burden of continued consequences. Want more proof? God's Word backs me up on this too. In 1 Thessalonians 5:16–18, we read, "Rejoice always, pray continually, give thanks in all circumstances; for this is God's will for you in Christ Jesus."

So have I always followed my own or God's advice? Do I fast-forward to acceptance when presented with life's challenges? Not always. Sometimes I can do the right thing because I know this is what you do to get to the other side of issues. But other times, I get in that negative attitude funk, dig in my heels, and stay there for a while. This usually means there are other things going on that are complicating my getting grateful, and it is almost always a negative emotion—like anger, guilt, shame, lack of confidence, worthlessness, or a host of other feelings that put up barriers to the acceptance process. But here is the good news: being grateful works on these emotions too!

Journal Prompts

1. Not another list of things to be grateful for—I wouldn't do that to you. How about a list of things that are getting in the way of you being grateful.
2. Where do these things come from?
3. Now … how about ten significant and real things you can be grateful for (see how I gotcha there?).

19

Acceptance

IT'S AN ONGOING PROCESS, NOT A DESTINATION (UNFORTUNATELY)

A woman once told me that she hated it when people said, "Tell me about your journey with cancer." She would tell people that there is no journey, because *journey* indicates that there is an end at some point … but there never is. When I heard this, I knew exactly what she meant. When I was diagnosed with cancer the first time and it was decided that I needed six months of chemo (which ended up being extended to nine months), my husband (boyfriend at the time) said that once I got done, we would have a big party to celebrate. But you know what? We never did. Because on the last day of chemo, they sent me home with my medicines to help with the next few days of side effects and an appointment card to come back in a month. My doctor liked to watch his patients closely for reoccurrence. I saw him monthly for a time, then moved to three months, and then six months. It's been over twenty-five years now, and I am still seeing my oncologist every six months because I have an idiopathic low platelet count (was it the chemo or something else—who knows?), and most oncologists are also hematologists, and they like to watch these things. And that is just fine with me. I like having someone check up on me because I too am concerned about a recurrence or a new cancer. I have this false sense of security that a blood test every six months will ensure nothing terrible sets up or that we will catch it early … even though neither one of my cancers were even the slightest bit flagged by a basic blood test.

What I learned is that the end is never going to come. Once a cancer patient, always a cancer patient. You learn pretty quickly that this isn't something that ends. Yes—even when you are years out, there is the knowledge that it can come right back, or something else can go wrong. Somedays I'm good with being a cancer survivor, and other times, I'm anxious about my health. Is that a bump or a lump, or is it normal? Is my headache just a headache, or should I be worried? During menopause, I experienced hot flashes and mild night sweats, which launched me into wondering if my Hodgkin lymphoma had come back because that is one of the symptoms. If I have a fever, I instantly speculate whether this could be the start of leukemia—which I am at a higher risk for because of the chemo. And then I worry about being anxious because too much cortisol has been linked to cancer, so I really need to stop being anxious. And anxiety is a sin; I should cast all my cares on him because he cares for me (1 Peter 5:7 paraphrased). So now we can add lousy Christian to the list. On and on my snowball grows!

I grew up with cancer—that of my younger brother's. He was two years old when he was diagnosed, and I was six years old. His battle with childhood leukemia was a significant part of my childhood. He is forty-five years out from his cancer, and he still goes back to St. Jude's Children's Research Hospital for a yearly checkup. Cancer has become a lens through which a great deal of my world is filtered. There can be some really wonderful results of this—like being grateful for every day, keeping my priorities in check, and making sure there is nothing left unsaid or undone, because life is short. It can go the other way too. I can fret about what might or might not happen in the future. I can focus on the ongoing side effects of cancer and its treatments (between my two cancers, I have a torso full of scars, asymmetrical mounds that are supposed to look like breasts, and disgusting regrown toenails from chemo fallout), the injustice of it all, or my lack of safety concerning my health. When I have bad days or scary moments, I try to remember all the things I have to be grateful for and the positive lessons I have learned. I also try to remind myself that it is okay to have anxious moments; when you're a survivor of something significant, it has a way of leaving some tender raw spots that get irritated occasionally. Just because it has been a long time doesn't mean those fears are gone. I often fall prey to thinking that I should be magically over it—it seems ridiculous to still be having trouble with this stuff now that I am healthy.

Unfortunately, I am fairly sure this is just how my life is going to be. I'm going to have good days, great days, and then some really lousy days with it. The trick is to accept this—it's just the way I process stuff. Will it always be like this? No—it has gotten better in lots of ways over the years. I have gotten older, and there is some wisdom and acceptance that seems to come with age. Additionally, some of my life responsibilities have changed. I don't have small children that I am raising anymore. Having a second and separate cancer stirred up some stuff for me, but I am working on getting it sorted and processed. Therefore, I disagree with the "cancer is not a journey" lady. It's a journey, because I certainly have been to the mountains and through the valleys in my trip ... and I'm still on it. I am really hoping that I don't have to circle back around on some of this fun-filled journey ever again, but I really don't get much of a say in it. I just keep trudging along, hoping maybe, just maybe, what I have learned in my journey can help someone else with theirs.

Journal Prompts

1. What are some high points on your journey, and what have they taught you?
2. What are some low points on your journey, and what have they taught you?
3. What bits of encouragement would you share with someone who is just starting their journey with something difficult?

20

Acceptance

EVERYTHING IS GONNA BE
ALL RIGHT ... SOMEDAY

Ever heard a song out of nowhere, but for whatever reason, it stuck with you? A song that is not on the Billboard's Top 40. No one has ever heard it, but it makes an impression on you. I have a song like that; it even ended up in my wedding. I first heard the song in the 1990 movie *Green Card*, with Gérard Depardieu and Andie MacDowell. The romantic comedy is about two people who enter into a fake marriage, one for a prestigious apartment and the other to stay in the US. I don't want to spoil it for you, but it does not turn out to have the predictable happy ending. The final scene is an emotional climax, where we learn that one has sacrificed for the love of another. The song being played is "Eyes on the Prize," by the Emmaus Group Singers, headed by Harry Stewart, who wrote the song while hopeless and struggling with a substance-use disorder. Little did I know in 1990, while I was sitting in the theater watching the movie, that years later it would become a theme song of encouragement and inspiration for me. I highly recommend that you look it up on the internet and listen to it. But be careful; this is a common song title. Make sure to get the right one. Here's the chorus:

Keep your eyes on the prize
Don't be dismayed
Don't be dismayed
Deep in your heart
You must believe
Everything is gonna be alright
Everything is gonna be alright
Everything is gonna be alright, someday
(Emmause Group Singers, H. Stewart, 1990)

When I initially heard the song, I didn't know the background of its conception. I just really liked it. When I was diagnosed with cancer the first time at age twenty-six, there were some people who wanted to pray for a miraculous healing. I told them to knock themselves out, but I just had this feeling that wasn't going to happen. Me and God … we were going to walk through this valley together. The second time around, I knew it then too. This was part of God's plan for my life. A really rotten part that I didn't want to go through, but nevertheless, here we go. The first time around, I had just started a new job. I had been employed less than a month and was still on new-hire probation. They could have let me go, no questions asked. Thankfully, they did not. The second time around, I was in my last push for tenure at my university. Would this derail me now, when I was so close to clearing a huge academic and career hurdle? Thankfully, I had been working diligently through my tenure period, and earlier publications and service work came to fruition.

Is there ever a good time for trauma or adversity? Is anyone ever just sitting around saying to themselves, "You know, I could squeeze in a terrible life event right now. Get it in, get it taken care of, and then move on with all the good stuff life has to offer. Go ahead, God, bring it on. I have an opening until next Tuesday." Someone once told me that if you really want to make God laugh, just tell him your plans. Fortunately, both times I went through cancer, I knew that I would be okay. I wasn't sure what all I would have to go through, how bad it would get, or if I would live, but regardless, everything would be all right. We can hold on to the promise in John 14:1–3:

Do not let your hearts be troubled. You believe in God; believe also in me. My Father's house has many rooms; if that were not so, would I have told you that I am going there to prepare a place for you? And if I go and prepare a place for you, I will come back and take you to be with me that you also may be where I am.

The worst possible outcome would be death. I certainly didn't want that, but I could handle it. I have a home in glory. There are loved ones there already waiting; it would be okay, no matter what. When you have a personal relationship with Jesus, all this life suffering stuff is just temporary. If you start here, that even in death things are going to work out, anything else is up from there. Does readily accepting this reality and knowledge make everything better? No. I still worry, ruminate, and struggle with my thoughts and the what-ifs on a fairly regular basis. However, remembering that "everything is gonna be alright … someday," sure helps me to stay as close to sanity as I can.

Journal Prompts

1. What is the worst thing that could happen in your struggle? Can you handle it? You might not like it, but can you get through it?
2. What is the most realistic thing that will happen in your struggle? What can you do, if anything, to ensure the best possible outcome?

Shock and Denial

SHOCK IS NOT ALL THAT BAD—JUST GO WITH IT

Shock is an interesting physical and psychological condition that represents an entire system reaction. Shock can initially feel very uncomfortable, like every system in your body is panicking. Symptoms might include a surge of adrenaline, a desire to come out of your own skin, feeling shaky or suddenly sick to your stomach, needing a trip to the bathroom, or feeling like the world stopped spinning and you are drifting … like something in a movie. All of these symptoms have fancy psychological terms to describe the panic that often accompanies bad news, crisis, or a trauma. The bottom line is that your whole person—mind and body—is shouting, *"Nooo!"* This is not a fun state! It feels physically and psychologically uncomfortable. Fortunately, it doesn't last forever.

After the initial digestion of the terrible news, some people struggle with feeling like a zombie. Just stumbling through their day, unable to focus, losing time, not remembering important bits of information, and not feeling entirely present. This is a form of disassociation, and it is not altogether a bad thing. It's a protective stage as you adjust to the news. After my mother died, I had to drive two hours to get back to my hometown alone. I have no memory of the trip … and I was driving. My father remembers little of my mother's funeral and for years after would ask me if certain people came to pay their respects. There are numerous neurological properties at work that account for the feelings of initial panic that change to surrealism. It may cause some people to seem to have no reaction. Where is the crying, sadness, anger, fear? It's all there. Don't worry. You'll have to deal with it all eventually, but if you're in the floating, "I can't believe this is happening," numb stage … just know that it's normal, because everything right now is abnormal. It is important, however, not to make any major decisions while in this stage and to surround yourself with people you trust to have your best interests at heart. When it comes to dealing with difficult situations, sometimes you just have to give yourself permission to be whatever you are for a little while.

Journal Prompts

1. What are you feeling right now? Describe the physical and the emotional parts of yourself.
2. What are the different thoughts bouncing around in your mind?
3. Remember that shock is biological and psychological, and it is a protective stage of adjustment. How might this weird, out-of-body surrealism be helpful to you right now?

22

Shock and Denial

BUT I FEEL FINE!

Both times I was diagnosed with cancer, I felt fine and was the picture of health. The first time, I found a bump (lymph node the size of a pea) in my groin area and decided I should get it checked. The pea-size bump was no big deal; it was the ginormous lymph node in my clavicle that I was unaware of that ended with the diagnosis of Hodgkin lymphoma. Later, I learned that the itching with no apparent cause I experienced in my neck and chest area was due to the cancer. I just thought I had dry skin. I was twenty-six years old. Then, at age forty-nine, I went in for my yearly mammogram … and got a call the next day. No lump or bump this time. It was a grouping of calcifications[2] the size of five grains of sand that ended with my breast cancer diagnosis. No other symptoms … no numb spot with coughing like Victoria Jackson, no nipple crust, discharge, or sores, no change in appearance or dimpling … nothing. My breast oncologist asked me twice, "Are you sure you didn't have any pain in your left breast?" Nope … I was just getting my yearly checkup like I do with my dentist.

---

[2] Quick note—calcifications are totally normal in breasts. It is not the presence of the calcifications that is concerning but the pattern and shape that can be a warning. Don't panic! Even if you do have a suspicious pattern, most of the time it is a much to do about nothing. And if, God forbid, it is something, you have caught it early and are in a particularly good place to be proactive and knock it out of the park!

Good news both times—I was healthy, which meant that I had a much better chance of doing well with my treatment protocol. And both times, I said to myself and others, over and over, "But I feel fine. How can I have *cancer*?" Even though I was thankful that my breast cancer was caught early, and I had several options for treatment, there was a part of me that kind of wished I had just skipped the mammogram. Ignorance is bliss in some situations; however, cancer is not one of them.

It is hard to go through medical procedures that make you sick when you are healthy. At twenty-six, I embarked on nine months of chemo—sixteen episodes of voluntarily allowing someone to inject me with medication that would render me exhausted and weak for the next week or so. Not to toot my own horn here, but I had decent breasts for forty-nine years old. My husband would agree with even more positive words of affirmation. He misses them too. We were in the parking lot of Panera when I heard that still, small voice and had a sudden assurance of what I needed to do—double mastectomy. With my health history, it was the only thing that would give me peace. To know I had done everything I could for it to not come back. No one could communicate to me with any kind of understanding how large the cancer in my breast was or where it was located. Apparently, calcifications are fickle red flags. But when they removed my "healthy" right breast—they found a speck of it in this breast too—7 mm of cancer still encased in the duct. Praise the Lord for chemo and double mastectomy, even though I felt fine and looked healthy. There is a real injustice knowing you have to do something you don't want to do, something that is not going to be fun, because of something you did not ask for—but sometimes you just have to do what has to be done. Well-placed superlative of your choice here_____. Four-letter words welcomed. I think Jesus gets curse words … he wouldn't use one, but I bet he gets our carnal need for one every once in a while. This is a bit of humor, folks. Please, no letters.

Journal Prompts

1. What things are going right in your life that are going to help you through your current mess? Work to avoid all the negative stuff. We all tend to give that enough attention without being prompted.
2. How can you take the stuff that is going right and magnify it in this challenging time?

23

Shock and Denial

I'M NOT READY FOR THIS—I
HAVE RESPONSIBILITIES

Is there ever a good time for adversity? Has anyone ever successfully bargained with God to have their trauma put off to a time when it was more convenient? I'm fairly certain the answer is a big fat no! As a professor of social work, I get to teach one of the best classes *ever*—Human Behavior in the Social Environment. This class helps students understand how we develop across the life span: physically, emotionally, mentally, cognitively, socially, and spiritually. If a significant life event happens to someone when they are four years old, that person will deal with it in a different manner than a forty-four-year-old. These developmental phases and dynamics across multiple life domains must be appreciated when working with clients. These countless factors also account for differences in how people react and process life events—positive and negative.

The expression of grief and loss varies across different life phases too. Sick children who are dying don't worry about death; they worry about the sad adults they are leaving behind. Teenagers who taste their own mortality through the loss of someone their age have an emotional reaction that can be difficult to describe or understand, by themselves or others. A mixture of egocentrism, realism, and the invincibility fable commonly causes teens to struggle in processing their issues. Older adults, on the other hand, often have an acceptance of death and may welcome what comes next. If you are an adult, however, grief, loss, death, or significant change is just inconvenient. I have responsibilities. I'm working, raising children, I have stuff to do! Jesse Ventura said it best in the 1987 film *Predator*: "I ain't got time to bleed!" But bleed he did (he also got eaten … sorry for the spoiler). Declarations of "I do *not* have time for this!" are just a waste of time and energy. Settle in, sweetie, and hang on—it's going to be a bumpy road.

But what you can do is gather as much support and resources needed to weather the storm—you also need to cut dead weight and baggage that is making your journey more difficult. This might be physical stuff—like chores at home or responsibilities are work—just for a season. After my surgery, I was on weight restriction of no more than ten pounds for six weeks. They tell you nothing more than a gallon of milk, but that's only eight pounds. I couldn't vacuum or mow the lawn for six months. Guess what? My son can vacuum like no one's business, and there are lots of other people who can mow the lawn. No one did a lick of laundry; I still managed to do this myself, but I had to have help carrying it to the washing machine and back to where it belonged once clean. The much harder stuff to collect or cut is emotional stuff. You and *only* you know what thinking processes you need to hold on to, embrace, and encourage and what thinking errors you need to purge and resolve to not entertain. Psalm 26:3–5 says,

> For I have always been mindful of your unfailing love
> and have lived in reliance on your faithfulness.
> I do not sit with the deceitful,
> nor do I associate with hypocrites.
> I abhor the assembly of evildoers
> and refuse to sit with the wicked.

We may need to cut out activities that are hurtful, emotions that are fed by lies and thinking errors, or people who are toxic to our current situation. This might sound harsh, but being strategic, logically and spiritually, affects the aftermath of your time of adversity. Like any journey or monumental feat—the better equipped and prepared you are, the more likely you are to complete the task successfully—even if you didn't plan this jaunt, even if you don't have time for it.

Journal Prompts

1. What are some supports and resources you have and/or need right now—physically, emotionally, spiritually?
2. What are some things you can farm out to others and step down from for a time?
3. What are some thinking processes that are helpful, whether secular or spiritual?
4. What thinking processes are holding you back and need to be cut?

24

Shock and Denial

IT IS WHAT IT IS, AND
I AM WHAT I AM

An important truth to appreciate in social work is that every client is different. In one of the classes I teach, we spend a great deal of time looking at some of the factors that account for these differences. Just like in class, vocabulary is important, because if we are all defining a term the same way, we are all on the same page. So indulge me here, will you?

Temperament. Characteristics that have defined you since you were born. Things like introverted, extroverted, easily adaptable, slow to warm in new situations, easygoing, and so on. You just show up this way to life.

Personality. The pattern of behaviors, emotions, and cognitive processes that someone develops as a result of their interactions with the world. One's personality is affected by numerous factors, including temperament, socialization, individual experiences, socioeconomic status, education, and many others. Once developed, one's personality is the most consistent aspect of a person.

Resilience. The ability to bounce back from difficulty. Some people come into this world with loads of resilience. Like the old Timex slogan, they can take a licking and keep on ticking. Others seem to possess very little resilience and struggle extra hard with life's difficulties. Here is the good news: unlike temperament and personality, resilience is something that can be purposefully developed.

Values. One's belief system that determines behaviors, priorities, and how one lives their life. Our values are significantly influenced by our family of origin; however, they can also change with education, experiences, and choice.

Worldview. The collection of one's culture, experiences, and values that informs how information about self and others is subjectively processed. This dynamic is fluid; it changes throughout life, in positive or negative directions.

These five items are complex dynamics that interact. It's like when different-colored balls of playdough are all squished together. While each color will remain intact and delineated, they cannot be separated from one another. If you understand all this, you can start to see why no two people are the same and why no two people are going to go through adversity the same way.

When I read personal accounts of how famous Christian women have tackled difficulties in their lives, I am amazed at how they seem to celebrate it all and come through it with a smile on their face while owing it all to their WWJD bracelet. I have women in my life who seem to never have a bad day. They're just high on the Lord and being grateful for this and thankful for that. And while I aspire to be like this, I am *not*! I am a sinner who can be ugly, resentful, and stubborn in my behaviors. And let me tell you, I bless *no one* when all this is spilling out of me, no matter how hard I try to suck it up and slap a smile on my face. But here is the thing. Some of this I simply will not be able to change. Some of this is the result of temperament and personality, and I'm kind of stuck with it. Thankfully, however, I can change the other three. I can choose to get my mind in the right spot and approach issues strategically to ensure the best outcome. Psalm 34:17–18 says, "The righteous cry out, and the Lord hears them; he delivers them from all their troubles. The Lord is close to the brokenhearted and saves those who are crushed in spirit."

Focusing on Jesus and his promises is going to yield much better results that allowing myself to spiral downward in the "woe is me" and "nobody likes me, everybody hates me, guess I'll go eat worms." I can choose to focus on the negatives of my world or the positives. It's all up to me. I have gone both ways. I have ridden the pink cloud of seeing Jesus in all my hardships, and I have gone down the rabbit hole of stinking thinking. Spoiler alert—there is nothing at the end of the rabbit hole that is redeeming or productive. Save yourself a trip and work with what you've got, and be intentional with the rest!

Journal Prompts

1. What are some things that you know about yourself that work against you when you're struggling?
2. What are some things you can do purposefully to counteract those items identified in journal prompt 1?
3. What is one thing you are going to do today to help yourself come through this difficulty in a positive manner?

25

Shock and Denial

I DON'T KNOW IF I CAN DO THIS

There are inspirational and moving stories in the Bible, something to go to for *whatever* issue you have. Sometimes, however, it might be hard to think of one when you need it. I have my favorites … but sometimes for different reasons than others:

- I love the story of the woman caught in adultery who is brought before Jesus (John 8:1–11). This just shows that Jesus was the first social worker and the biggest liberator of women *ever*!
- The Good Samaritan (Luke 10:25–37), which is a testament to Jesus being all about diversity, inclusion, and equality.
- The prodigal son (Luke 15:11–32), because we have all been the lost one who needed grace to come back. Also, because I am a middle child, I totally and completely get the brother who feels utterly unappreciated!
- Jael (Judges 4:17–24), because sometimes women just have to take care of business!

There are many more, but one that I often think about is Hosea and Gomer (what an unfortunate name, eh?). Found in the Old Testament, this is a story of a man (Hosea) and his unending love for his wife, a former sex worker, who repeatedly keeps going back to her old ways. What I think about is Gomer at the end. She is all used up, too old to catch a husband, too old to trick, being sold at a slave market … likely at bargain basement prices. In Bible days, slaves were displayed naked, so the buyer could get a good look at what he was buying. Considering that Gomer was a naked woman with a bad reputation and the battle wounds of sex work, three children, and the aging process, you know there were some glares, unkind words, and perhaps some unwanted touching and prodding. I imagine that when she was standing there waiting to be purchased, she had the thought of *How did I end up here? What in the world is wrong with me? Why can't I do anything right?* But then love comes walking in (thank you, Sammy Hagar and the rest of Van Halen, for such a great song). Hosea shows up and redeems her … *again.* Don't you know people looked at him like he was foolish and advised him against having anything to do with her. Not to mention, Gomer likely didn't feel that she deserved it. Personally, I think this is why Gomer kept leaving Hosea and returning to her old ways, because she didn't think she deserved to be treated well. Trauma can be complicated and complex, which can make for extremely poor decision-making and head-scratching activities. There is a clinical term for it called *paradoxical behaviors,* and it means to react in counterproductive ways. Paradoxical behaviors set up vicious cycles that keep going and spin faster and faster in the wrong direction, making things far worse.

The problem is that these things don't just stop. Even with realizations and insights, remnants remain. You have good days and bad days, and just when you think you have it licked, your unresolved issues will show up with a fury to remind you they are still there—kicking butt and taking names! Even resolved issues like to resurface and get a hold on you. So what is a person supposed to do? Something intentional that you know (not *feel*—feelings will lead you astray in these situations) is in the right direction. It might be calling a trusted soul and telling them your struggle. It's amazing how verbalizing what you are thinking and feeling can take away some of its sting and power. Writing it down and keeping it or burning it. Listening to positive music, watching a funny movie, going for a walk, exercising, reading the Bible, praying … just do *something* that moves you in the opposite direction. To borrow from Alcoholics Anonymous, "Just do the next right thing."

It's my hope that when Hosea got Gomer home that last time, she was able to start the process of making peace with her issues. Maybe she tried a ladies' Bible study, took up baking bread, yoga … whatever worked for her. We can logically deduce that something got her going in the right direction, because we don't hear about Gomer anymore. While God did radically change her life, she still had to go through it—even when she didn't think she could, not for one more moment. Hang on and be purposeful, and trust that in time, it will all be revealed.

Journal Prompts

1. What issues seem to keep coming back and causing you problems?
2. It's important to have a proactive plan to deal with these things, because when you are in the middle of it, these ideas don't tend to come to mind. What are three to five things you know would help you turn your thinking and behaviors in the right direction?

No Stinking Thinking

TIME TO GET A TRASH CAN

Have you ever cleaned out a junk drawer, especially one that is crammed full of stuff? Some things you need, others are just junk you should have thrown away and never put in the drawer, and then there are the items that were okay when they initially went in, but over time, they have turned into junk. All you can do is pull up a trash can and start going through and culling the junk from the good stuff. Occasionally, we need to do this with the thoughts that run around in our mind. Because, like the junk drawer that is so cluttered with unneeded stuff, it becomes a hindrance.

When dealing with negative life events, you need all the help you can get, and stinking thinking is not helpful. Actually, it's the exact opposite—it can be quite harmful. But for some of us, we like to hold on to stinking thinking items like a hoarder to junk! What exactly is stinking thinking? Stinking thinking is another name for cognitive distortions, which are internal thoughts that are not accurate but have been sparked by something external that was likely unpleasant. Cognitive distortions or stinking thinking (whichever term you like best) increases negative feelings about self and others. Because these ideas are internal, the only person who can cull through them to determine which are true and which are lies or junk is *you*.

There are additional issues to consider with stinking thinking. As humans, we like to engage in something called cognitive conservatism, which is the tendency to seek information that conforms to an existing self-concept. If we hold on to stinking thinking ideas about ourselves, we will also start to find evidence to confirm these ideas, moving them from falsehoods to perceived truths about ourselves. Simultaneously, we dismiss evidence that we are worthy and made by God with a mighty purpose. Like the junk drawer, accumulation of junk doesn't happen overnight—it takes time. A couple of stinking thinking ideas here and there, and in time, you find yourself with more junk than goodness, and that is a dangerous place to be, my friend … a most unhelpful and purposeless place.

How do you clean out the stinking thinking in your head? The same way you do the junk drawer—you go through it and trash what is not needed. Here is a four-step process to try:

1. Decide to be purposeful with what is real truth and what is junk. This is not a time for feelings, because emotions are not accurate sources of information about truth.
2. Change the stinking thinking self-talk. Grab a notebook and do the following:
    a. Make a list of the *facts* (example: I am child of God; I was made for a reason; I have strengths, such as … ; even my weaknesses are for a purpose).
    b. Make a list of the *irrational* (example: no one cares about me; I'm ignorant and can't do anything right; I'm worthless; people wouldn't miss me if I were gone).
    c. Correct the irrational statements with helpful and true statements.
3. When those stinking thinking ideas start to pop up, you purposefully and intentionally, aloud or to yourself, speak truth to the incorrect ideas.
4. Rinse and repeat as needed.

Sounds simple, right? Just follow these four simple steps, and the junk drawer of your mind will be cleaned out, and you will be as good as new. Oh, if only it was that easy! This is a process and one that you have to engage in often. But here's the rub—when you really need to purge the stinking thinking is when you are least likely to do so, because this is when the stinking thinking seems to make sense. The misery that it causes seems deserved, and the internal beating up of yourself is an attempt to punish and shame you into being a better person. But it never works—it only loads up more unhelpful and damaging stuff that is going to have to be cleared away someday.

Journal Prompts

1. Make some time to engage in steps 1–4 listed above.
2. When working on step 2, which was the hardest for you—a, b, or c? What does that tell you (and remember—*no stinking thinking here*)?

27

No Stinking Thinking

CHARACTER DEFECTS, WE ALL GOT 'EM! (PART 1)

I was a clinical social worker for more than two decades before I became a professor of social work. The bulk of my clinical work was in substance-use disorder circles, which also means mental health issues, unresolved trauma, highly dysfunctional support systems, and maladaptive coping skills, just to name a few challenges clients faced. I tell my students that I struggle with imposter syndrome about being a professor because I have terrible spelling and no matter how hard I try, I just make lots of mistakes on class syllabi and lecture materials. I struggle remembering and pronouncing names correctly, especially students with similar-sounding names like Sharon, Shannon, and Shawna. I jokingly tell them that these are character defects that just come with the package that is me, and it keeps me humble.

One dynamic of recovery from any significant issue is identifying and embracing your character defects. Character defects are those flaws that just seem to come with the person. We all have them—some of us are just more open to admitting them than others. No matter how hard we try, they are simply part of who we are. Everyone's list is different, but what all character defects have in common is they can be significant internal and external obstacles to our recovery efforts, and they really like to eat our lunch when we are struggling. Here is a short list of common character defects:

Quick to anger	Stubbornness	Selfishness
Dishonesty	Defensiveness	Playing the victim
Blaming (self/others)	Prideful	Slow to warm
Unforgiving	Resentful	Overly critical (self/others)
Pessimistic	Closed-minded	Impatient

There is likely little that one can do to completely change a character defect. You can work around it, but it is likely something that you are always going to have a bent toward. But if you know this about yourself, you can identify it, see where it is causing problems, and make more effective decisions about your behaviors, thinking patterns, and the words that come out of your mouth. Knowing your character defects can help you to understand certain barriers that make your journey seem more difficult than someone else's. Big disclaimer here—character defects should not be a crutch that you rely on like a get-out-of-jail-free card. Like any barrier, you have to figure out a way over, under, around, or through the issue. Also—and this might sting a bit—most other people, even those people who really know and love us, rarely account for our character defects when they are struggling to deal with us, usually because they are bumping up against their own character defects. Oh, the layers of our complexities!

Journal Prompts

1. If I'm being honest, I struggle with these character defects:
2. How do your character defects create challenges with difficult situation(s)?
3. Just for today, let this awareness marinate. Any insights?

28

No Stinking Thinking

CHARACTER DEFECTS, WE ALL GOT 'EM! (PART 2)

Hopefully, you are picking up this reading after you have read part 1. If not, or if it's been a while, please take time to go back and refresh yourself.

In part 1 of this discussion, we explored character defects. Those flaws that seem to just come with a person—part personality trait, part temperament, and all problematic! These are not traits that we boast about; oftentimes we find them embarrassing and shameful. Oh, and did I mention that we usually have several, not just one? Some character defects run in dynamic duos, like intolerance and impatience, or terrible trios, like stubborn, prideful, and jealous. One of my character defects is unforgiveness—and I hate this about myself. As a Christian who depends on God-given forgiveness and grace daily, I am stingy giving it to others. Why? I have no idea. I could engage in endless self-analyses, or I can just accept this disappointing flaw and know I have to work with it.

One other really frustrating thing about character defects is that they have the worst timing! When you are going through a challenging time, the last thing you need are more barriers and challenges—but that is when character defects like to show up! Unfortunately, I had a person in my life whose own character defects were overflowing into her attempts to help and support me—and it was coming out as all kinds of hurtful and offensive statements and negative behaviors. As a result, I felt hurt and began to harbor a great deal of resentment toward this person, which I allowed to put me in a dark place at a time I could not afford to be there. Even as I write this, I can taste the disdain I have to fight hard against so I don't go there again. It is an ugliness inside myself I dislike, but I can't ever seem to get rid of it completely. However, the intentional and purposeful part of myself reminds me that nothing good can come of this. I once again have to forgive her, whether I feel like it or not, or I am setting character defects up to take over … and no one wants that, especially me. The good news is, even though you might not be able to get rid of character defects, you can absolutely take their power away through awareness, intentional thinking, and purposeful behaviors. Some wisdom from God is essential too. Proverbs is chock-full of verses that speak to our need for wisdom. Check out Proverbs 2:6, 11:2, 13:10, 16:16, 17:28, and 19:8.

I worked on this issue of unforgiveness. I chose forgiveness, and it was better, and my feelings of hurt and anger abated … for a minute. But when I had bad breast cancer days—that sometimes turned into bad breast cancer weeks—guess what was right there, standing at my front door with their ball ready to play? You guessed it—unforgiveness and all the inconsiderate stuff that had transpired. While this occurred months ago, it was as fresh as when it first happened. I tried to explain it to my husband, but he, who does not struggle with unforgiveness, couldn't go there with me. He would say things like, "It was a long time ago," "I'm sure she didn't mean it that way," "She doesn't realize how she is coming across," and "She has her own unresolved issues." What I heard was "You are wrong, and I'm taking her side." What I should have done was told my husband that I didn't feel supported. I should have explained that it didn't matter what or why or how—it hurt! What I did instead was stop talking and let unforgiveness back in to stay for a while. It's funny how character defects can feel comforting and make for great company. Unforgiveness and I could go hours talking about all the thoughtless things this person had said to me and her insensitive behaviors. We talked about great ways to get her back and delighted in all the problems she must deserve. But after a while, I could see that by letting unforgiveness back into my life, all I was doing was setting myself back. It was straight up sin, knowing and willfully not forgiving someone … who honestly likely didn't mean the things she said to me, nor did she realize how she was coming off. But here I am again … right back to square one. But I'm going for imperfect progress, not perfection, so once again, I chose forgiveness. Once again, I intentionally work this process through. I sent unforgiveness and its ball away, but it will likely be back and at the absolute worst time, because this is how character defects roll. But I know these things, and God and I can work on it together.

Journal Prompts

1. What are the character defects that have been creating problems with your current struggle?
2. What can you do to work around your character defects? Hint—it is usually to do the opposite of whatever your character defect is.

No Stinking Thinking

LISTEN ONLY TO TRUTH—
THE REAL TRUTH

The human mind is an amazing machine that neuroscientists themselves admit they don't understand well. It is a vastly complex organ responsible for basic life functions, emotions, temperament, personality, memory, body movement, how trauma and adversity are processed, and more. Although all the parts of the brain may be labeled and we have the anatomy figured out, how all the parts play with one another remains a mystery. Another thing that the brain is responsible for is truth, specifically our truth about our world. While truth is supposed to be reality and facts, when it comes to our subjective truths about self, they are highly fallible.

Self-truths are those things that we believe to be true about ourselves, our lives, and others with whom we interact. They are based on our experiences and how we decide to reflect on these events. If we're not careful, we can get a negative and inaccurate idea going on in our minds. It sets up camp, and before long, it's taken on a life of its own. This is a common phenomenon that occurs when we are not checking out these ideas with someone and we are not filtering them through a lens of Christ. Let's look at some classics.

Error. As a young teen, you feel awkward and different due to puberty and the onslaught of romance. The object of your crush doesn't like you back, so you decide that you are ugly, undesirable, and if you only had the right clothes, hair, and bigger or smaller body parts, you would have caught your crush.

Truth. There is always someone better looking ... and worse looking. We were all made differently because humans are made with a variety of attraction templates—those things that make chemistry between couples. Crushes rarely work out, despite what we see in romcoms. If they weren't difficult, they wouldn't be called "crushes."

Error. I'm six years old, and my caregiver physically abuses me. They are the adult; they know more than I do. I depend on them for safety, love, shelter, food, and clothing, so they must be right. Therefore, I am wrong and bad and deserve the abuse I receive. As I grow up, I gravitate toward people who abuse me as well, because my truth tells me this is what I deserve, and it seems so familiar, it must be what is meant for my life.

Truth. It is never a six-year-old's fault that they are being physically abused. Adults have big problems that have nothing to do with their children; however, their children get the spillover. It is not fair, it is not right, it is not deserved, and it should be stopped.

See how this works? You take an event in your life, you make an incorrect assumption about it, and it becomes your perception of yourself and how your world works. Then you start to see things that reinforce your perceptions but discount or dismiss information that counteracts your inaccurate truth. It doesn't take too long or too many subjective reinforcements until an error becomes a distorted truth—and now *your* truth.

When dealing with a difficult or adverse event, you are especially vulnerable to thinking errors. But it's important to use a truth monitor that is not of yourself. Running it through the Christ filter can help you see real truth. Thinking errors are lies, and John 10:10 says, "The thief comes only to steal and kill and destroy; I [Jesus] have come that they may have life, and have it to the full." Right there—it is *not* the Lord's plan for his children to live in lies and thinking errors. What would Christ say about the truths you carry around about yourself? Are they really truths?

Journal Prompts

1. What are some thinking errors that you need to examine through a Christ filter?
2. What would Christ say about your subjective truths? What would his truth be?
3. How would your life be different if you adopted and listened to only real truths?

30

No Stinking Thinking

NOT YOU AGAIN

Good days and bad days … we all get both. Sometimes we understand why. Perhaps it is a situational issue that we celebrate or lament. Sometimes it is a physical feeling of being well rested or being so tired that petty things that would normally not bother us reduce us to tears. But then there are the other days. When an issue you feel like you have made some progress on seems to just come out of nowhere and says, "You thought you'd seen the last of me … Ha! I'm back." Ugh! The truth of the matter is that some rotten events in our lives are like bad pennies—they keep showing up.

After my breast cancer, I had significantly more negative emotional garbage to sort through than after my lymphoma twenty-three years prior. There are lots of reasons why that are sprinkled throughout this book. I felt like I had made great progress on issues—put them to bed with the right attitude and spiritual resolve—only to wake up and be struggling with sadness, anger, or disappointment. As a professor, I grade a lot of papers, and one particular day, I couldn't stay focused long enough to get through a single student assignment … and it wasn't because they were poorly written. I found myself looking up breast tattoos. Not 3-D nipples … that would not help my center-stage, four-inch-long scars on each mount where a breast used to be. I was looking at tattoos that covered the scars. Some were huge, ornate pictures and designs; one photo was of a tattooed lingerie bra. Then I came across a photo of a vine where the scar was with flowers and buds in various stages of development emerging, and I howled. What was it about that picture that took me to my knees? It was because I wanted this part to be over! I wanted to grow and move past this … this wounded feeling. The pity pot and the ongoing feeling like I was in this alone! Why did this keep coming back around? I was healthy now! I was so fortunate to have survived two cancers. How many people did I know who had died of terminal cancer? If you find yourself in the middle of a bad day and you are asking yourself questions similar to these … I'll go ahead and give you a spoiler: there are no answers coming. Not today anyway.

Here is the good news: bad days end. Sometimes you just have to ride them out and start fresh in the morning, and other times, you can make the intentional decision to end it in its tracks. Second Corinthians 10:5 says, "We demolish arguments and every pretension that sets itself up against the knowledge of God, and we take captive every thought to make it obedient to Christ." Stinking thinking is completely and totally unproductive—it has no redeeming merit—so why spend one more minute ruminating in it? Because for some of us (myself included), stinking thinking can be like a blanket we like to get all wrapped up in, because that's just how we process stuff.

Journal Prompts

1. What are some of the stinking thinking thoughts going on inside your head right now?
2. Are any of these thoughts productive? Helpful? Getting you anywhere? Why or why not?
3. List productive thoughts and ideas that can chase away the stinking thinking.

Anger

KÜBLER-ROSS ... YOU DON'T KNOW JACK!

Lots of people are familiar with the five stages of grief coined by Elisabeth Kübler-Ross: denial, anger, bargaining, depression, and acceptance. Kübler-Ross's 1969 text, *On Death and Dying*, is the accepted treatise on the subject and is commonly a required read by those getting degrees in the social sciences. According to Kübler-Ross, when someone is subjected to a significant loss or crisis, or is anticipating a terminal event, they may go through all or some of these five stages. It is important to remember that there is no starting point in the five stages, no rule that says you must pass through each stage in a prescribed manner, and it is also possible to go through two or three stages and then come back around and go through a previous stage again. The most foundational lesson of Kübler-Ross is that it's a process, and no one is going to go through the process the same way and in the same fashion. There is a reason that Kübler-Ross's model has stood the test of time—its' good stuff that makes logical sense, and there are hordes of people who can identify with her stages.

I have taught Kübler-Ross in several classes. Again, solid stuff all future social workers should know. However, I personally like a lesser-known model for trying to understand the process of grief and loss—the Westberg Model. Granger E. Westberg, in his book *Good Grief* (1962), identified ten stages of grief and loss and explained how these stages manifest themselves across physical, emotional, cognitive, and behavioral domains. Basically, he took Kübler-Ross and added the phrase "It's more complicated than you might think." This is a picture I use when discussing Westberg to students, and I think it accurately describes most anyone's struggle with significant adversity:

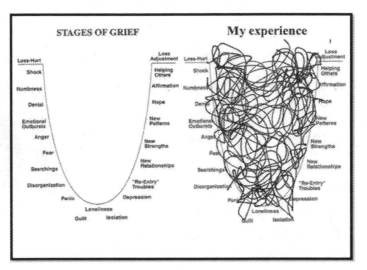

Stages of grief—my experience

My first time around with cancer, I honesty did not have to go through some of the Kübler-Ross or Westberg stages. But my second time around … oof!! I hit every stage at least once and seemed to get stuck like a pinball between Westberg's anger and loneliness for longer than I care to admit. Why did I struggle more the second time? I'm still not sure. Maybe it is because at forty-nine years old I had a lot more to lose. When I was twenty-six years old, I was new in my career field, single, and unrooted. The world was my oyster, and this was an unexpected speed bump that I could take on and then live my life. But by the second cancer, I had a life, a wonderful husband I wanted to grow old with—like *gross* old, two beautiful children I was not done raising, rites of passage into adulthood to celebrate with them, future marriages to help plan and attend, and *grandbabies*! Comedian Jeff Allen says, "Everything they told me about grandchildren is true: they are the reward for not stabbing your sixteen-year-old." I was in the best career of my life and one year away from being able to go up for tenure at my university. And listen—I could write another book about my journey to academia—an "uphill both ways" story of rejection, waiting (and I do not wait well), and self-doubt. For a kid who was called unintelligent and "slowpoke" in first grade by her teacher, who spent a summer learning how to reread between second and third grade (thank you, Mr. Huddleston), and having a third-grade teacher tell me years later, "My goodness, Dana, I never though you would graduate high school, let alone get a college degree" to be on the cusp of tenured professor and to be diagnosed … are you serious with this right now? So yes, for all those reasons and many more, the Westberg Model resonates with me. Perhaps you too. If so, just know these models are there because adversity, trauma, grief, loss … they are all journeys. Miserable, stinky, unfair, "I didn't sign up for this," "why me," "not now," "I think I'm going mad," and "I don't wanna" journeys. God gets unpredictable and wild journeys, and he knows that we are in need of comfort in the process. Psalm 34:17–18 says.

> The righteous cry out, and the Lord hears them; he delivers them from all their troubles. The Lord is close to the brokenhearted and saves those who are crushed in spirit.

Journal Prompts

1. What phases of Kübler-Ross and/or Westberg do you identify with? Are there any that you feel stuck in or seem to keep coming back around to?
2. Why do you think you are stuck where you are?
3. What can you do to intentionally get unstuck if you are in a stage that is unhelpful to you? If you are in a healthy spot, how are you going to stay there?

32

Anger

PEOPLE ARE IGNORANT

When I was diagnosed with breast cancer, I was showered with love and support from many people. People committed to praying for me, sent cards with words of encouragement and Bible verses to remember, and, of course, sent food! We Baptists like to feed people, especially in difficult situations. However, I also encountered some really hurtful statements and inconsiderate behaviors. I was appalled because these were things I would never say or do to someone. Would you like to hear some of the worst?

"Poor Alan [husband]. He shouldn't have to go through this with you *again*. That's a lot to ask of a person, and frankly, it's not fair to him."

"I hope Alan's not a breast man, because this might be a deal breaker for him. Just be ready. He might leave you over this."

"You are so lucky! You get to pick out a new set of girls and look like a teenager again. I kind of wish I would get easy breast cancer so I wouldn't have to pay for implants."

"Do you really get to say you have cancer if you don't have to have chemo? I mean, you're getting off so easy and everything with just having surgery."

"Thank you for your interest in our support group, but you do not have a significant enough presentation to be invited to join the group at this time."

This one is my favorite. Well, not really. *This* is the one that stunned me the most:

"You know, you're not a woman anymore now that you don't have breasts."

Even more difficult to understand was most of the insensitive words and actions came from people I thought would be some of my go-to supports. If I put on my social worker hat and compartmentalized my feelings, I could see that when people said these inconsiderate and inappropriate statements to me, they were actually trying to help. I tried to keep this in mind, but some days it was really difficult. As the one dealing with cancer, I had enough to deal with; I did not need people's insensitivity and ignorance too. But just like when someone steps on your toe, they can say they are sorry, but it doesn't make your toe stop hurting.

My husband and I have a saying: people are ignorant. It's an empathic statement we say to each other when someone has done something that is irresponsible, frustrating, insensitive, or hurtful. The definition of "ignorance" is to show a great lack of intelligence or common sense. I would say that this is what I encountered, and as an avoider of conflict, I just took it on the chin and kept going, then ruminated over it later. At some point, it doesn't matter what people say or do; it matters what you do with it. Some people can easily let stuff go, while others are keeper and compounders of injustices. But holding on to that trash, all it does is continue to create problems. Ephesians 4:29–32 gives a clear warning about hurtful statements and grudges:

> Do not let any unwholesome talk come out of your mouths, but only what is helpful for building others up according to their needs, that it may benefit those who listen. And do not grieve the Holy Spirit of God, with whom you were sealed for the day of redemption. Get rid of all bitterness, rage and anger, brawling and slander, along with every form of malice. Be kind and compassionate to one another, forgiving each other, just as in Christ God forgave you.

Journal Prompts

1. What are some hurtful and/or insensitive statements or events you have experienced around your time of struggle?
2. Reread Ephesians 4:29–32. What does holding on to these moments of injustice look like in your world?
3. What would happen if you just let them go? What are the benefits?

33

Anger

NO ONE GETS TO TELL
YOU HOW TO FEEL

Have you ever heard the saying "Those who can't, teach"? Not to sound arrogant, but I do not think that this applies to me. I was a clinical social worker for twenty-one years before I became a university professor—so I would say this is evidence that I can do social work. However, I learned a great deal about my profession as a professor; someone has to read those textbooks. One of the classes all social work students must take in our program is SW 221 Interviewing Skills. It's known as the rite of passage class for social work students. True to this label, we lose students almost every semester because they come to realize during this class that social work is not for them. The class is co-taught, and the first time I had the privilege of teaching the class, I got to sit back and learn from the master herself—Kathy Miller. She and another instructor had developed the class years before, and over the years, she had become the expert. I brought my legal pad and pen to class every day and took more notes than the students did. I never had a class in all my education matriculation devoted just to interviewing skills. I learned a lot of my skills on the fly and through trial and error. One thing I realized *very* quickly was that I had picked up some unhelpful habits and was flat out doing some stuff wrong all those years.

One lesson all students learn is to remove the phrase "I understand" from their repertoire of empathic phrases. Because no one can ever completely understand what an adversity means to another person, even if you yourself have gone through the same thing. You might be able to relate to what someone is saying, you may have even struggled with the same emotions and thought processes, but it still doesn't mean that you understand. We all come to life with different lived experiences, temperaments, personalities, and worldviews; therefore, we are all going to have our own take on life events. So instead of saying things like, "I totally understand where you are coming from," we teach students to provide comments that communicate "I heard what you are saying, and I validate what you are feeling." This is where real empathy comes from, and this is what feeds a hurting soul and allows for partnering toward change. Here is the other problem with "I understand": it's commonly followed by "because this is what happened to me ... blah, blah, blah blah." The focus moves from the person hurting and now is all about the speaker. This does not communicate empathy; this says, "My story is more important than yours."

The next phrase we teach students to avoid is "Well, at least." We have all done this; trying to make a person feel better about their lousy situation, we offer up a more positive spin to their circumstances. "You're in a domestically abusive relationship, and Children's Division placed your children in foster care? Well, at least you know your kids are in a safe place." When you utter the phrase "Well, at least" to someone who is hurting and struggling, you invalidate them. You are essentially telling them, "Don't feel that way." Well guess what, Sherlock? I'm already feeling that way, and now I can just add frustration and feeling like no one gets it to my troubles.

Maybe this is why, when I was diagnosed the second time, I struggled with some of the "support" (notice the quotation marks) I received. I found myself in a sea of "Well, at least they found it early ... Well, at least you only have to have surgery ... Well, at least your kids aren't little and don't really need you ... Well, at least you're healthy ... Well, at least COVID is not as bad so you can have your *elective* surgery" (notice the italicization), and on it goes. Well-meaning people saying things that did *not* validate me. Then there were the "I understand" statements. "Oh girl, I understand completely." To which I wanted to scream, "Oh really? You've had cancer twice before the age of fifty? You had a younger brother who was diagnosed with leukemia at the age of two and grew up going to St. Jude's Children's Research Hospital? You had to see a therapist in seventh grade because of your irrational fear of cancer? You have been haunted by cancer for what seems like your whole life, even though every birthday candle and eyelash wish was 'Please don't let anyone in my family get cancer, including me'? You understand that I deal with remnants of my first cancer and now I'm going to lose both breasts and will have additional scars to remind me daily that my body continues to fail me? You understand what it is like to lose your nipples and know that since that is a big part of getting to the finish line during sex that I may struggle with intimacy with my husband? You understand all that and more, do you?"

But I didn't. I just smiled and said thank you, and walked away feeling dejected, unvalidated, and unimportant. SW 221 had spoiled me. I wanted more. What I wanted was someone to tell me that whatever I was feeling, I had every right to it, and it was a rotten hand that I have been dealt. The first time I was diagnosed with cancer, I called one of my best friends who was four hundred miles away and told her I had Hodgkin lymphoma. To date, she said the most validating and poetic thing anyone has ever said to me. "Well _____ (appropriate superlative here)." Exactly! She said what I what I was thinking, and I thought, *Yes, somebody gets it without judging me or trying to make me feel better about it.* Someone was raw and real with me, and it made all the difference!

Now ... before you start judging me, let me say this. I know that I had countless things to be thankful and grateful for through my trials. Most of those good-hearted "Well, at least" statements were true—I was healthy, I didn't have to have chemo a second time, my kids were older, both cancers were treatable, I live in America, and I have health insurance. The list goes on and on. I also know that dwelling on the negative is unproductive, dangerous, and counterproductive. But sometimes you just want someone to hear you ... to validate you where you are and just be with you in that moment for a time. Then, and only then, do they have the right to give you the much-needed kick in the pants to get moving in a different, more productive direction.

Journal Prompts

1. What do you wish someone would say to you about your situation? What would validate you to the core?
2. What well-meaning but ill-timed statements can you now see have merit?

34

Anger

CUT 'EM ... SERIOUSLY

Difficult situations are full of surprises. They can be amazing events that reinforce that there is a God in heaven and he is in charge. Then there are other events that are so strange and bizarre that you might catch yourself saying, "Seriously ... I have never heard of anyone having to deal with something like this." I had unbelievable stuff happen both times I went through cancer. With my breast cancer, I was outraged at the hurtful and inconsiderate statements women shared with me (read about it in "People Are Ignorant"). However, when I had Hodgkin lymphoma, I had not one, not two, but three people who attempted to befriend me to help provide them with legit information to feed their factitious disorders of cancer. One person was obviously faking to get attention and perhaps a date. Another one was doing it under the guise to get some fast money. Both of these people were spotted for what they were quickly. But the third, wow, she was a doozy, and she even had her husband going for months. Those of you who have taken a class in abnormal psychology might want to diagnose her with Munchausen syndrome, but once it all broke open, it became clear that she was conning people to avoid her husband filing for divorce, being fired at work, and being prosecuted for embezzlement ... and just in case you are thinking this was a good idea, it wasn't. Her husband did divorce her, she was fired as she was being arrested at her place of business, she did go to prison for embezzlement, and she impressively burned a number of bridges.

She and I were in the same Life Group (a.k.a. Sunday school) at church, and I assume she hatched her plan after seeing the loving support and response I received when I was diagnosed with Hodgkin lymphoma. Not long after, she announced she also had cancer, and we quickly bonded over our common plight. At first, we would compare our symptoms and treatments, as well as some of the side effects we were experiencing. But after a few weeks, I started to notice that things were not adding up. She cut her hair super short, but her hair was not noticeably thinning like mine. I started to look like a cancer patient; she did not. She didn't know the name of her doctor and never had the telltale signs of IVs, blood draws, or chemo push infusions. Her husband didn't know anything about her cancer either and was not permitted to attend her treatments or appointments. The story goes on and unraveled in glorious form, but the bottom line is she was found out—she was faking cancer, and I felt violated, duped, and utterly perplexed. Cancer at twenty-six was not enough? I had to have this madness happen too? The same thing later when I seemed to have a slew of women saying such hurtful things to me. I would think, *What did I ever do to people to deserve this kind of treatment?*

Here is the answer—nothing. I did nothing to deserve this kind of treatment because others' bad behavior has nothing to do with me. With the faker, she obviously had serious mental health and criminal-thinking issues. With the hurtful women, it's a mixed bag. Some were trying to help but were off in their assessment of what makes for encouraging words, and one was so jaded by her own bitterness of unresolved issues from her own breast cancer journey that it just spilled out on to everyone—not just me.

Regardless, what is important is to remove yourself from it. When you're struggling with difficult situations, you can't afford to have negative people and their issues further complicating your life. Sometimes, you just have to walk away. Metaphorically or literally, separation can be healthy. It's like cutting off a diseased branch to save the tree. It's dangerous for you to allow people with a negative influence to be a part of your journey through a difficult situation. Second Timothy 2:16–17 says, "Avoid godless chatter, because those who indulge in it will become more and more ungodly. Their teaching will spread like gangrene." Sometimes this means telling a person you need to part ways for a time or permanently. Other times, you can simply avoid or limit your exposure to certain people. It may be the healthiest thing to do in a complex time of your life. When you are struggling with difficult circumstances, it's like waging a battle, and you have to be strategic with your resources. Protecting your physical, emotional, mental, cognitive, and spiritual environment is important to getting to the other side. Once there, perhaps you can circle back around and deal with negative people or process it for what it was, but for today—you may just need to cut them loose.

Journal Prompts

1. Identify negative people in your world who are unhelpful to your journey.
2. Could an open and honest conversation help the situation? If so, what should you say to this person/people?
3. If an open and honest conversation is just going to make things worse, how could you avoid or limit your exposure to this person/people for a while?

35

Anger

WHEN ALANIS MORISSETTE
IS VISCERAL

Have you ever scared yourself with your own anger? It's embarrassing and shameful to say, but I have. Interestingly, it happened while I was driving. One afternoon, I was minding my own business, driving down a back road to try to get to a nearby town faster than going through the city. I was scrolling through XM Radio when I came across "You Oughta Know" by Alanis Morissette, at the beginning of the song. As a child of the eighties and nineties, I decided to stop scanning and listen. There was nothing else that had piqued my interest, and I only go to music when there is nothing good on the comedy stations. I knew this was a song of anger—pure and raw. Years later, it would be revealed that Morissette wrote it after her relationship with David Coulier (a.k.a. Uncle Joey from *Full House*) ended and she felt hurt and jaded. So how is it that as I drove down this back road—a fifty-year-old woman in a wonderful marriage—I had such a visceral reaction that I cranked the volume and kept a death grip on the steering wheel as I was screaming the lyrics with tears blurring my vision? Because of these lines:

> And I'm here, to remind you
> Of the mess you left when you went away
> It's not fair, to deny me
> Of the cross I bear that you gave to me (Morissette 1995)

Suddenly, this song was not about a breakup but my unresolved anger at Christ and others in my life who seemed to have abandoned me in my cancer journey. Logically, I know this is not true. I can see the hand of God working before, throughout, and after cancer—versions 1.0 and 2.0. I can list numerous people who sent me cards, made me a meal, or sent me text messages of encouragement. However, what I felt for the majority of my second round with cancer was that no one cared—including the Lord. I know that is heresy and that I risk being struck by lightning to even write it … but that is what I felt.

Here is the thing about emotions and feelings—they are *not* accurate barometers of what is actually happening. One of the biggest trappings I found myself in was comparing my first cancer experience to my second. My first time around, God carried me—his presence was palpable. But the second time, if felt like he was nowhere to be found. I also felt like no one in my support system was really all that concerned either. During the crisis of the event, I was all business. No time for grief, just move forward with what sadistic remedy I needed and deal with the emotional part later. The mental part didn't really start until complications with my reconstruction became apparent. It seemed so unfair to me that my mounds were so janky looking. Before breast cancer, I never struggled with asymmetry, but now I had one D cup (due to encapsulation) and one C cup that showed all the implant ridges due to the fat graphing being reabsorbed. By this time, it was four months later, the crisis was over. I'm healthy, and everyone has forgotten what I went through. No one asked me how I was doing or mentioned my cancer. I had my time in the limelight, and now it was over. But I was just getting started on all the nasty stuff … and there it was in the Alana Morissette song: "It's not fair to deny me of the cross I bear that you gave to me."

So what did I do? Likely the worst thing—I decided I was done. I would take care of my own grief counseling and postcancer support. No more bringing it up. I cried when no one was looking, I slapped a smile on my face, isolated when I could, and I started keeping track. How long would it be before someone noticed or asked me if I was okay? Professionally, I knew this would not end well. What I craved and needed was a support group of other women who I could relate to and give me the "been there, done that" wisdom. But it was COVID—all support groups in my area had been canceled. Online support groups were available, but when I applied to be in one, I was told that I did not have a significant enough presentation to be admitted. They had to limit the number of participants, and I was being told what I felt like the rest of the world was telling me, "You are healthy. You didn't have chemo. You don't need support." Being rejected by a support group does something to ya! It was a terrible and lonely place. I felt insignificant, unworthy, and unwanted. And worse, I had plenty of evidence to back up my thinking errors.

Spiritually, I also knew this was not the right path to take. Ephesians 4:26–27 says, "'In your anger do not sin.' Do not let the sun go down while you are still angry, and do not give the devil a foothold." Are you hoping for a final paragraph of how I got myself right out of that funk? Well, sorry to say, it took about eight months before I saw my way through this particular stage. I let many suns go down on my anger, and boy oh boy did I let Satan eat my lunch! I learned a great deal about myself, but one of the most foundational lessons is I needed to tell people I was struggling. Pride goeth before a fall. Well, in my case, I had to fall, tumble down some rocks, get pretty skinned up, and even then, I didn't ask for help. By the time I did, it felt too sacred to share. Hence … the book you are reading. Just for the record, I do not recommend going about dealing with significant life issues in this manner!

Journal Prompts

1. What do you need right now to feel supported? If you are getting all you need, write about how wonderful it is to have this area fulfilled. If not, what would you like to receive from someone else? How could you go about communicating that need?
2. Music is an incredibly powerful generator of emotion—positive and negative. What are some songs, groups, or genres that you know are good for your mental health? Identify what the right song can do for you. Maybe today, spend some time listening to uplifting music.

36

Injustice, "Why Me," and Pity Pot

BUT I HATE PINK

I knew I was in trouble when the nurse practitioner called me. Let's face it—they let the front desk ladies tell you if your test results are good news. Then she started with asking me about how I was feeling and if my biopsy incision site was healing properly. Double trouble; she's stalling. Finally, she got to it. "Okay, Dana, well, unfortunately your biopsy came back positive for cancer ..." and that was about all I heard for a few moments. I even had to say, "Stop. Can you start over and say everything again?" *Cancer ... again ... and I am not even fifty years old yet.* There was also a series of superlatives that came to mind, but I was able to keep those to myself.

I took down as much information as she gave me over the phone, asked about next steps, made sure I had the correct spelling of ductal carcinoma in situ (DCIS), and thanked her for calling. Then I hung up and thought, *But I hate pink!* Pink—the color associated with breast cancer. It was good for a slight smile in a horrible moment. Oh, did I mention that I had to leave class to take the call? I had to go back in and teach out twenty minutes of a university course. Only with the strength of the Lord, but we did it.

Truth is I avoided pink because I had this magical thinking that if I didn't like pink, I would never get breast cancer. Absurd, right? But these are the cognitive mind tricks we play to give ourselves a false sense of safety. And now my safety net was gone, and I felt exposed and scared … and angry … and the victim of a great injustice. I already had my cancer journey. When I was twenty-six. Was Hodgkin lymphoma, nine months of chemo, and all the side effects that came with it not enough? Now I have a secondary cancer? Are you kidding me right now? Shouldn't it be someone else's turn? I never really struggled with the "why me" my first time around, but I was struggling with it now. "Why me *again*?" Because in my world, if you have already had cancer once, you're done—you get a bye for the rest of your life. Additionally, research shows that only 1–3 percent of cancer survivors develop a second cancer different from the original cancer (Livestrong 2021). However, that is simply not the way it went for me. And as a result, it's time to adjust the thinking. It could be bad luck and just a coincidence, but if I approach this situation with that thought process, it is not likely going to be very productive. But what if I decide that there *is* a reason, a purpose, something to come from this other than the negative stuff. First Peter 5:10 says, "And the God of all grace, who called you to his eternal glory in Christ, after you have suffered a little while, will himself restore you and make you strong, firm and steadfast." God has a reason for this to be part of my story. Camping out there … now that might just be the way to go.

Journal Prompts

1. What are some magical, irrational, or unproductive thoughts that ruminate in your brain about your situation?
2. How could this negative event be something that actually has a positive purpose?
3. Since you have to go through it, what do you want God to do with this situation that you cannot?

37

Injustice, "Why Me," and Pity Pot

FAIR? BETTER LUCK AT
THE COUNTY FAIR

When adversity strikes, there is a good chance that at some point you will hear yourself think, feel, or say, "It's not fair." Hopefully, there will not be someone standing there with a quick and unhelpful retort about the county fair in the summer. You may also tell yourself that you are not a little kid anymore and that it is childish to hear yourself say, "It's not fair," because nothing in life is fair. But here it is. You ready for it? If you are thinking, feeling, and/or saying it, it is real to you. For a minute, just look at a couple of definitions. In the world of social justice, *justice* means fairness. Simple, right? But look at the definition for *injustice*—coercively established and maintained inequalities, discrimination, and dehumanizing development inhibiting conditions of living imposed by dominant social groups, classes, and peoples upon dominated and exploited groups, classes, and people (Smith-Barusch 2018). Significantly more complex, eh? You may also be asking yourself, "What does this have to do with what I am going through?" Injustice, lack of fairness … it's all about power, and when you are struggling with adversity, it may seem like your power has been taken by whatever trouble has come into your life. Therefore, instead of focusing on "it's not fair," how about focusing on taking your power back? And the best part? You don't have to wait until the county fair comes to town in the summer.

What exactly does taking back your power mean in adverse situations? It means being purposeful with how you think about things, what influences you allow into your life, and what things you move out intentionally. Colossians 3:2 says, "Set your minds on things above, not on earthly things." When you are having a day of "it's not fair," I would challenge you to think about someone else's plight in life who is struggling with palpable injustices. When I was a practicing social worker, sometimes I would have a bad week, filled with difficulties, frustrations, long hours, and lack of appreciation. It was easy to fall into a negative attitude and complain about my job. But then a client would come in with a humbling story of adversity that no one should have to suffer, and I would think, *Goodness … my life is wonderful, problems and all.* Our sense of injustice due to struggles is real, but do we need to feed it? Sometimes you do—and you go right ahead and vent and process how unfair your situation is. But once you are tired of being there, a purposeful change of focus allows you to regain control and power over how your adversities make you feel.

Journal Prompts

1. What are the injustices you are struggling with right now?
2. What are three self-statements you can come up with that allow you to regain power from your adversities?
3. Where do you want to camp out in your mind right now—and why?

38

Injustice, "Why Me," and Pity Pot

NOBODY CARES

You have likely heard the lyrics of the song by Sean O'Boyle, saying, "Nobody likes me, everybody hates me, guess I'll go eat worms." This is supposed to be a funny children's song, but there are times when this might feel very real. We're especially vulnerable to this line of thinking when we're going through a challenging time and not getting the support, care, or magical fixes we would like. If you ever hear yourself think or say aloud, "Nobody cares about me or my problems," just know you are sitting on that unproductive pity pot. Why that pity pot is so alluring and comfy, I'll never know. But here are three truths about getting too comfortable on the pity pot: (1) if you stay too long on it, you will create a self-fulfilling prophecy; (2) others will grow tired of your behavior, because people who get stuck on the pity pot are tiresome and off-putting; and (3) others can see that you are on the pity pot, but you are the only one who can pry yourself off. Ouch … did that sting a bit? Sometimes the truth does.

As a professor, I point out lots of grammar and formatting mistakes in my students' written assignments. One of the common mistakes I point out is to avoid using polarizing language. Things like "always," "never," "the fact is," "everyone knows," and so on. In the world of social work, because we work with people, and everyone is different, there is rarely a situation where these polarizing words are appropriate. The phrase "nobody cares" is one of those polarizing terms that is inaccurate.

There are people who care. Admit it. They are out there. So what is really going on when we feel like this?

I know that this feeling is true. This was my subjective and inaccurate self-truth for a time with my second round of cancer, and I still have to fight this thinking error when it comes around from time to time. For me, the real issue was not getting the support that I needed … nor was I asking for it. I was already angry at the fact that I had to go through this cancer garbage again, have my breasts cut off, and deal with all the unpleasant stuff one had to deal with—a medical community that treats you like cattle, insurance companies that get to make medical decisions, the waiting, which is the worst, the inconvenience of it all, and people who say well-intentioned but really inconsiderate and sometimes flat out inappropriate things. I expected people to magically know what I needed—to read my mind. Additionally, I didn't want to admit I was angry. It made me feel like a vulnerable and weak person, and it was embarrassing. I was struggling with feeling like I didn't have the right to be angry with God; look at all the wonderful things he has done and is doing for and through me. I have cancer, yes, but operable cancer. I am going to be fine; I am not going to die. I am so much more fortunate than others. Whether or not I should have been angry, I was indeed angry, and I needed someone to relate to me in this. However, I put on a rather good poker face, and no one saw this. Instead of realizing that no one knew I needed help because I wasn't telling anyone what was really going on, I began to believe that no one was looking. I became even angrier, and now I was starting to pull away from those who did care, and in my mind, it was completely justified and warranted.

Why is it other people can hear our stinking, error-filled thinking a mile away, but when you're in the middle of it, you can't see the forest for the trees? If you're feeling like no one cares for you and your difficult situation, I can tell you, with almost certainty, that you are wrong. Is it possible something else is getting in the way of you feeling cared for in the way that you need? Do you need to reach out and make it known that you need help? Why is it so many of us struggle with this when research shows that people desire to feel needed, to serve as a confidant, and to partner with people in challenging times? Now hear me when I say this: you need to be wise in who you approach for support.

Trustworthy people who have your best interest at heart. What would happen if we simply approached someone we know who cares and said, "I'm struggling with _____, and I was hoping I could process some stuff with you"?

Journal Prompts

1. Make a list of people who care about you. Remember, it is okay to list loved ones, friends, professionals, and organizations that you might not go to for help, but those people who you know care, think, pray, and/or love you.
2. What is keeping you from reaching out and getting the support you need?
3. Look at that list in prompt 1 again. Who on that list can you approach for some needed support?

Injustice, "Why Me," and Pity Pot

DANGEROUS PLACE TO BE

I had an amazing mom, but we still had a complicated relationship. Standing 5'1", with the smallest feet of any adult I have ever met, Judy Smith was the most assertive woman in my life. She often threatened to get a chair out if needed to smack my brothers and me across the face. She did not put up with disrespect or dishonesty, and she did not play when it came to discipline. If she put out an "If you do _____, this will happen," you had better take heed because she would follow through. My mom was one tough lady. As a girl, it was discovered that my mom had a hole in her heart, and if it was not corrected, she would have been significantly disabled by the time she was an adult. At the age of twelve, my mother had experimental heart surgery, and, praise God, it was successful. Now remember, this is in the 1950s; open heart surgery on a child is not common like today. They went in through her back, which left a huge crescent-shaped scar. The surgery halted her growth, and she was left with a compromised cardiovascular system that decreased her endurance for physical activity. Additionally, the anesthesia used in her surgery later caused pulmonary fibrosis, limiting her ability to effectively move air. However, my mom never let these things stop her; they slowed her down, but she kept going. Therefore, she did not have much patience for those who struggled with the pity pot.

Most people who are treated for stage III Hodgkin lymphoma have twelve chemo treatments; this was, and still is, the standard protocol. However, when I completed my twelve treatments, my oncologist suggested four more—just to make sure, because the only area of disease I had after my initial biopsy was behind my breastbone, and it was less evasive to give me more treatments than to crack my breastbone and do a biopsy in a secondary location. To hear that I needed four more treatments when I thought I was done was heartbreaking. I was already making future plans, secretly hoping there would be a wedding in my near future. Not to mention I was tired and struggling from the twelve treatments I had already endured. I had just a scant of hair left, I had gained considerable water weight, my hormones were all out of whack, I had lost my toenails (which was way worse than losing my hair), and I was exhausted. My toxicity level from the chemo was accumulative, and I couldn't imagine four more treatments worth on top of what I already had.

They ordered my chemo cocktail, and I got my thirteenth treatment, fighting back tears (not successfully) until I could get home and have myself a good cry. About ten minutes into my cry / pity pot session, my mom, who had come into town for what was supposed to be a celebration of being done with chemo, entered my room and said, "Hey, your dad is putting down some landscaping rock in the front of your house. You should go out and help him." I was incensed! "What? I just found out I have to have more poison dumped into my system and derail my life even more than it already has been, but you think that I need to go do manual labor with my father?" And this is what she said: "Well, lying across your bed crying isn't getting anything done, and come Sunday, you are going to feel terrible and be in bed all day, so I think you probably need to get up and get some stuff done around here."

That was my mom. Always moving forward and no time for moping. I will tell you that it was not her wisdom that got me off the bed and outside to help my dad; it was my anger at what I considered her insensitivity to my situation that got me motivated. And as I was outside helping my dad with yardwork, contemplating all these things in my mind while displaying quite a nasty attitude, something dawned on me. She was right. Being active, doing something, staying busy was helping me to process my setback more quickly than lying across my bed with the "woe is me" ruminations. And, true enough, I was on a clock. I had about thirty-six hours before the chemo was going to put me down, and I needed to get stuff done. Before long, I was feeling much better emotionally. I was checking off my to-do list and feeling productive. If my mom had not given me the mental kick in the butt I needed, and I had hit my hard chemo days after being on the pity pot all that time, I would have been in a very dark and dangerous spot. You stay in one place too long, you run the risk of becoming too familiar and getting stuck there. And let me save you the suspense—getting yourself unstuck is not easily done!! You may be familiar with Psalm 23:1–3, "The Lord is my shepherd, I lack nothing. He makes me lie down in green pastures, he leads me beside quiet waters, he refreshes my soul. He guides me along the right paths for his name's sake." There is something to notice with this passage—it's action orientated. This verse is about movement, doing something, not getting stuck in one spot.

Journal Prompts

1. What are the unhelpful pity pot thoughts and complaints that you struggle with?
2. Are these thoughts and complaints helping you or encouraging you?
3. What can you do when these thoughts and ideas start setting up camp in your mind? Make a long list of productive thoughts and physical activities you can engage in instead.

40

Injustice, "Why Me," and Pity Pot

I DO EVERYTHING RIGHT, AND LOOK WHERE IT GOT ME

I'm a pretty healthy person. I'm not the health nut who can say that she hasn't ingested refined white sugar in over a decade, but I am privileged enough to be able to eat a healthy diet full of fruits, veggies, and lean meats. I exercise almost daily, and my blood pressure numbers, BMI, and blood count numbers are good. Yet I have had two completely different cancers before the age of fifty. After surviving Hodgkin lymphoma, I made the recommended changes in my diet. I have never been a big meat person—if you take me to a buffet, I go for the side items—I'm a "fixins" kind of gal. Therefore, avoiding nitrates in processed meats and soft cheeses was not difficult for me. I love soy products, have never consumed alcohol or used recreational drugs, and water is my favorite beverage! If you go through the risk factors for breast cancer, I only check one—intact ovaries. Yet, I still got it. Think of all the bacon I passed up, and for what?

I still struggle with this sometimes. As a social worker who worked in substance-use disorder treatment for nineteen years, I have seen many clients who abused their bodies terribly yet were for the most part physically healthy. Remember, I only saw them for a short season in their lives, and I know that in time, hard living catches up to all of us. But it just seems so unfair sometimes—an injustice! To deny myself the fast food and yummy, albeit unhealthy foods and drinks and still get a second cancer. Seriously!

Or … perhaps living a healthy life is what got me to forty-nine years old before my second cancer showed up. Women far younger than me develop breast cancer for no evident reason or risk factors. And perhaps my healthy lifestyle is one of the reasons that I came through my double mastectomy as well as I did. I came home the same day and walked down the street and back before I went in the house. I walked a mile by day four and was able to do all my own post-op care. Maybe having cancer at twenty-six drove home the need to be healthy so I can avoid other medical issues in the future. It really is all about perspective. Ephesians 5:20 says, "Always giving thanks to God the Father for everything, in the name of our Lord Jesus Christ." Perhaps being grateful and thankful for the privilege of access to healthy foods, medical care, and accurate health education should be my focus, because believe me, there are a lot of people who do not have this trifecta … and that is a true and real injustice.

Journal Prompts

1. What are some of the thoughts that make your difficult circumstance seem unfair?
2. What about the flip side? What are some positive ways to think about it?
3. Sometimes, things are unfair—you have been dealt an injustice that no one should have to face. But how can your intentional perspective help you move forward?

41

Sadness

IT'S A LEGIT TEARJERKER

Some stuff in life is just sad! There are lots of synonyms for sad, like unhappy, disappointed, mournful, sorrowful, dejected, downhearted, and so on. But all these words have something in common—they're no fun! There is a time for every emotion in life. Ecclesiastes 3:1 says, "There is a time for everything, and a season for every activity under the heavens." If you read the next seven verses, the Bible provides a rundown of it all. Sadness is one of the emotions that is part of God's human condition, especially in the wake of difficult news, trauma, adversity, or loss. There are some pitfalls with sadness. On one side of the continuum, you have the problem of getting stuck in it. Sadness becomes a tar pit, and, like the saber-tooth tiger, you can get bogged down and exhausted. Unsticking yourself is not easily done. It takes a conscious and intentional change in your actions and cognitions to accomplish this. You do what you need to do, even if it feels like the last things you want to do. It's like physical therapy; it hurts at first, and you question if it is doing you any good at all, but then slowly you start to see progress and realize that each day, you are a bit stronger than yesterday.

But then there is the other side of the continuum. The side filled with thinking errors that you are not allowed to be sad. That somehow showing the emotion of sadness is something you must hide because it will make you look weak and/or it will be difficult for others to watch. With everything else going on in your life, you feel pressure to protect others from your realness. Another thinking error concerning sadness is that it makes you look like a bad Christian. Spiritual bypass is the tendency to use spirituality as a means of avoiding difficult feelings. An example of this would be to deny feeling sad by focusing on God's plan for your life. Spiritual bypass can be a helpful coping technique; however, it can also create unresolved issues that eventually are going to come home to roost.

Jesus experienced sadness. He wept when his friend Lazarus died, creating the shortest verse in the Bible, John 11:35. He cried tears of blood hours before his earthly death. I'm sure that Jesus was legit sad about what was about to happen—crucifixion, rejection, and unimaginable pain. He was also leaving his twelve disciples, his mother, his believers, and his earthly ministry. He didn't apologize for showing sadness, nor did he feel that he needed to justify his sadness to anyone. It just comes with the territory, people!

While I can write a devotional about the sadness trap, I have also struggled with the thinking errors that come with it. I had a mother who was not one to lick wounds. She was a "get up, dust yourself off, and let's go" kind of person. Therefore, not stopping for sadness was modeled and encouraged when I was a child. Sadness can seem unproductive and a waste of time. I also fall prey to spiritual bypass, expecting myself to be content in all circumstances, delight in God's will for my life, and rejoice in the increase in my faith that will be coming. While focusing on these things is helpful and puts us in a better place mentally and spiritually, it is also okay to just be bummed. It doesn't help that friends and family members try to spin sadness as a means of making us feel better. While this can remind us of more positive concepts to soften the difficulty, it also sends a message—don't be sad. When I decided to have a double mastectomy, I got some of these messages:

"Well, at least you won't have to wear a bra anymore" (actually, not true—if you have reconstruction, it is recommended that you still wear a bra ... and for the first six weeks, it's a bra 24–7 with compression garments).

"Be thankful that you are having something cut off rather than removed internally—it will be easier" (yes ... *easy* is the first word that comes to mind when I think of a double mastectomy).

"No more mammograms for you … lucky" (I would much rather have real breasts and a yearly mammogram, which is quick, easy, and painless. Good gravy, what is wrong with people?).

Sometimes, what we want and need to hear is this: "What you are dealing with is straight up sad, and I can handle the emotion if you need to be real with someone." Jesus can certainly handle the sad … been there and done that!

Journal Prompts

1. What are you sad about concerning your situation?
2. If a friend was struggling with sadness in a comparable situation, what would you tell them?
3. Are you stuck in the sadness, or do you need to be in the sadness for a minute? What is your next move?

42

Sadness

VULNERABILITY IS HARD
FOR EVERYONE

Few things in life make us more uncomfortable than viewing a loved one's physical and emotional vulnerability. If you're an athlete in a fierce competition, spotting a vulnerability is a golden opportunity to be strategic and earn an advantage. But when you love someone, it's like seeing them in a stage of undress. You're not meant to see it, but it is beyond their control. I think the best word for it is *exposed*—totally and completely exposed.

Most of us work hard to avoid exposure of our vulnerabilities. And don't be disillusioned; we all have things we don't want other people to see! Some of us even have secret pacts with a family member, shovel friend, or lawyer that if something happens to us suddenly, there are things that must be done immediately to keep secrets secret (by the way, this is not a healthy thing—but that's another book). My mother put us all on alert that when she died, she did not want an open-casket viewing—actually she wanted to be cremated, for several reasons. But I remember her saying, "Don't you dare let people walk by and look in on my dead corpse. I do not want this to be what people remember about me." I feel the same way and have also alerted my family. No amount of mortician magic can cover up death, and I would much rather people remember me as a whole, living person, not someone hidden beneath pancake makeup and processed into a view-ready state.

However, when you are going through difficult times, be it a life event, illness, or trauma, sometimes vulnerabilities are front and center for all to see. You've got bigger fish to fry, so you just don't have the time, energy, or wherewithal to keep stuff covered up. Oftentimes, when our vulnerabilities are flapping in the breeze, we feel extra sensitive to the judgments of others, real or imagined. This can add extra negative layers to what we are already dealing with, and we certainly don't need anything extra in a time of crisis. Here is what I know about vulnerability as a social worker—it comes, then it goes, and in time, it fades from memory.

My grandfather was a high school basketball star—tall and good-looking in his youth. A strong and independent thinker, he was a real man's man. He could make tough decisions when no one else would, was generous with his time and resources, and was a protective husband and father. Toward the end of his life, however, he struggled physically. He was on dialysis, labored to walk more than a few feet at a time before his legs would hurt, and lost some of his basic physical dignities we all hope to hold on to, no matter what. When he passed, those final images haunted me. His vulnerabilities that I knew he didn't want anyone to see but was unable to conceal due to his need for constant care. Are you sad, reader? I'm sad writing this, with tears in my eyes … but hold on—it gets better. These images, they fade. With time, grieving, and healing, those images of his final days were replaced with the grandfather of my childhood. A strong and healthy man who loved to fish and hunt and who had the work ethic of John Henry. It's part of the process, and the vanishing of the vulnerabilities and the replacement of the healthy and happy memories is a sign that you have made it to the other side.

Sometimes we try to hide our vulnerabilities from God. There are several people in the Bible who tried as well: Adam and Eve, Abraham, Gideon, and Jonah. They each had what they thought was a good reason, but in the end, it was a fruitless effort. It's pointless to try to hide anything from God; he sees and knows all, and he can handle it all. In the world of social work, we believe that secrets keep us sick. There is a great deal of freedom in being real with God. Once we admit what we are struggling with, regardless of how shameful, guilt ridden, ridiculous, or silly it may make us feel, God can handle it. This is why

Christ came—to liberate us! Once we are open and honest with what is really going on, all that energy we had tied up trying (not successfully, I might add) to keep our vulnerabilities secret is now available for processing, healing, changing, and applying for a different tomorrow.

Therefore, when it comes to God, let it all hang out. I promise you don't have anything God hasn't dealt with before that his grace can't cover. Additionally, there is no limit to the grace. John 1:16 says, "Out of his fullness we have all received grace in place of grace already given." There is no set amount that you get and once you are out, you are just out. No rationing needed, no saving for later, and no making sure that only the really bad vulnerabilities are the ones you bring forward. There is more than enough for all. No matter your prowess for getting a good bargain, this is absolutely the best deal ever.

Journal Prompts

1. What are some vulnerabilities that you try to keep away from others?
2. How do you think other people would handle the real you—secrets and all?
3. How do you think God handles the real you? What differences do you see between journal prompts 2 and 3?

43

Sadness

EVERYTHING IS CHANGING

Adversity, trauma, and demanding times bring lots of emotions. As humans, we come equipped with a barrage of feelings, a full spectrum from glorious to horrible. We tend to favor a certain area of the spectrum. Some people are optimists and see the glass half-full, while others spend the majority of their time on the pessimist side. As well as lots of emotions, adversity also brings with it change. Oof ... change!

Good news—Hebrews 13:8 tells us that "Jesus Christ is the same yesterday and today and forever," so we have that to hold on to. God is not going to change on us. But everything else is free game. And even if the change is good, it is still stressful because it requires an adjustment. Change brought on by adversity is rarely celebrated—or at least not in the early hours of it. It may also bring dark emotions—feelings of injustice, anger, frustration, fear, and sadness. Changes connected to adversity mean saying goodbye to things you don't want to lose—innocence, sense of safety, relationships, body parts, and perhaps your existence. Additionally, adversity has its own time schedule, and it does not care if it is inconvenient for you. You might also notice that change likes to happen in a cluster with other life events, when it feels like this is the last thing you need right now. No wonder most of us do not welcome or delight in change!

When I was diagnosed with breast cancer and decided to have a double mastectomy, I went to the internet to see if I could find some before-and-after photos. This was a sobering experience. My initial plan was to have a skin-sparing double mastectomy, keep my nipple, and do the reconstruction at the same time—the one-and-done surgery. However, when I communicated this to my breast oncologist, she shook her head no. While it is possible to have the surgery I wanted, rarely does a woman qualify for it. I started out with lofty expectations and ended up with, "How about two appropriate mounds under a shirt? Can we do that?" The more I learned what was ahead, the more disheartened I felt. During the crisis of the event, I pushed it all aside because I needed to get this done and I could not get a surgery date fast enough. There was healing from the first surgery, drains, and lots of follow-up trips to the doctor. Each time, they would say how great I looked … to which I would think, *Really? If this is good, what does bad look like?* Then there were tissue expanders, a second surgery to exchange my expanders for implants, more healing, and I was done. Except I wasn't. I had so much scar tissue that I lost some of my range of motion in my left arm, so I had to go to physical therapy for several months. Good news—I got it back (you really do have to do the exercises they send you home with). Then it became obvious that one of my implants was encapsulated because one mound was rock hard and larger than the other—noticeably. The remedy for this? A complete redo, with drains and everything. When I asked if I would look significantly different, I was told, "Hardly at all. We can't even guarantee you won't encapsulate again." As of the writing of this book, I am still trying to figure out what to do. Change, change, and more change … and not in the direction I was hoping. Disappointment and sadness are part of the deal sometimes. Eventually you have to pivot and adjust. The ability to adapt and change is what keeps humans at the top of the food chain, but that doesn't mean it is easy, natural, or fun. Give yourself permission to be sad because what you are feeling is legit. But you also have to know when to push on and leave sad behind. Pivot, adjust, move forward, and get started on your new normal.

Journal Prompts

1. What are some changes that have come with your difficulties?
2. If you are struggling with sadness or disappointment, why?
3. Whatever is on your list, own that it is legitimate—these things create negative feelings, or at the least, stress. But how can you now adjust and move forward?

44

Sadness

SOMETIMES YOU JUST NEED TO LICK YOUR WOUNDS FOR A WHILE

I bet you have heard true and touching war stories involving dogs or seen photos where a trusted canine will not leave his/her fallen service person's side, up to and including the handler's funeral. Dog and soldier companionship, dependency, and respect for each other has a long history, with dogs being a part of war from the beginning of time. Dogs and the unwavering loyalty they show is central to some soldiers' healing process from visible and invisible wounds. One such dog was Sallie, a lifesaving companion during the Civil War. She is honored with her own monument at the Gettysburg National Military Park Museum and Visitor Center. If you haven't been, I highly recommend it, and if possible, be on the open battlefield at dusk. For just an ephemeral moment, you can picture what it might have looked like in 1884. Sallie is honored for many accomplishments. She was raised by the Eleventh Pennsylvania Infantry from a puppy and brought happiness and normalcy to her company. She would remain with fallen soldiers, giving them comfort in their most terrifying moment; she was proudly introduced to President Lincoln, and she is buried in the hollowed grounds where she died after being shot in battle (Ebert, n.d.). She also was a licker of wounds.

I have a friend who works as a nurse in a wound care unit. She tells stories that have me looking for a trash can as I try to hold back the gag reflex. Her department employs all kinds of nontraditional methods in an attempt to heal stubborn, antibiotic-resistant wounds. Hyperbaric chambers, topical applications mixed with sugar, maggots, and increasing protein in a patient's diet have all been shown to help when nothing else will (note that this is not medical advice—for discussion and illustration only). I grew up in the country, and if you allowed a dog to lick you, you ran the risk of developing intestinal parasites or some other germ-based yuckiness. I love dogs, but no doggy kisses for me please. Dog saliva, however, contains antiseptic properties that when applied to a wound can provide a barrier, decreasing bacterial growth and infection. Civil War Sallie knew this, which is why she would lick the wounds of her soldiers; she was working to provide them protection and time to heal so they could live to fight another day.

When tragedy and adversity come our way, sometimes we might need to lick our wounds for a bit. Take a minute to sit with what has happened, admit it is a difficult situation that will create a disruption to your equilibrium, and acknowledge that it stinks. Yes—life is hard and filled with ups and downs, and everyone is going to have to go through some challenges, but that doesn't mean that we have to hide that we are affected. There is a time for a brave face, and then there is a time to just be real. When I had cancer the first time, it was just me. Single gal, living alone. I could be whatever I needed to be because I had lots of time to myself. The second time around, I had two children I had to protect. I knew that they would take their cues from me. If I was optimistic and calm, they would be too. If I was scared, anxiety ridden, and angry, they would likely follow with their own negative emotions, or worse, take on the role of parent to me. I could not handle that kind of role reversal, so I put on a brave face, I worked hard to spin all the positives I could, and I reassured them that while it was cancer, it was going-to-be-okay cancer. I would survive with minimal treatment. I would have a couple of surgeries and be just fine. "Please don't worry about me; this is just a speed bump in life and, really, not a very big one at that. Your daddy and I have this covered, so please don't worry."

I did this same thing with my father and siblings. They did not need to worry about me; they all had their own problems, for goodness' sake. I also did this at work. "The timing is perfect," I assured my program director, department chair, and dean. "I am going to have my mastectomies and reconstruction during the summer, and I will be back in time for fall semester like nothing happened. I can still work on my tenure dossier, publish academic work, and prep for a full slate of classes." And I did. I was so good at convincing everyone that I was fine, it is no wonder that no one noticed when I started to struggle. I even had people tell me, "You make cancer look easy."

Looking back now, would I have done anything different? No. I am glad that I was able to be optimistic and tackle cancer with a determined and strategic plan that eased those around me—because cancer affects others too. I am glad that I was able to spare my family some worry and concern, or at least I hope I did. I am glad that work didn't bat an eye and continued to treat me like every other faculty member.

But what I do regret is not telling people that I was struggling. I waited too long. I isolated and didn't let anyone in on what was going on in my head, and then when I was so full of anger and ugly resentment that I couldn't take it anymore, it took people by surprise. When I should have been needy, I worked really hard not to be. Now I had an emotional wound that had not been cared for, and it needed special attention because it was resistant to the normal course of treatment. We have already discussed the debacle of being rejected by a support group for lack of significance. This called for professional help. And that is how I ended up in an online therapy session ... and for the first time in over a year felt heard. This is what my wound needed to finally get a jump on real healing.

Another regret—I wished I would have found a counselor sooner and not waited so long. Lots of people have hang-ups about therapy, but no one refuses medicine when they are sick—because there is obviously something not working that needs outside help. Therapy can do the same thing. Proverbs 11:14 says, "Where there is no guidance, a people falls, but in an abundance of counselors there is safety" (ESV). If you are working to process and transcend your issues, and you are struggling with reoccurring issues that are resistant to what you are trying, perhaps it is time to call in a professional.

Journal Prompts

1. What are the barriers in your journey of healing?
2. Where do you think these barriers come from?
3. What might be something different (and positive) that you could do to get a jump start on your healing?

Sadness

THE WHAT-IFS

I'm a planner. Be it what are we going to eat for dinner while we are eating lunch, what we will serve our guests on Saturday night, or what we will need for an upcoming vacation, I always have a list going that I seem to add more to than I get to cross off. My plan is to have all my Christmas gifts bought before Thanksgiving (although, no matter how hard I try, it never works), and I strive to have all my course preps completed for the entire semester before the first day of class. I have a lot of daily goals, but rarely do I actually get them all completed.

I am also a planner when things go wrong in my life. I learned that I come by this naturally, as my dad is also a planner. My mother passed away in May 2014, but before she died, she had several brushes with death. One of these times, my dad and I were sitting in the special family room of the ICU—not the main waiting room, but the smaller, private room where you never want to be because it means your loved one is in bad shape. My dad looked at me and said,

"She doesn't want a funeral."

"Okay, we won't have a funeral; we will have a celebration of life."

"She wants to be cremated; do you think you kids can handle that?"

"Of course, Dad. We all know that she doesn't need that body anymore. We'll honor her wishes."

Our conversation would have gone on with other plans to be made, but one of my brothers, who is not a planner, could not handle the conversation, so we tabled it. I knew instantly what my dad was doing—planning for how he would deal with losing my mom. *What if she dies? Where do we start? What if she gets better but can't come home? Which assisted nursing home would be best for her? What if this is a long-term hospital stay? Should I go home and sleep or should I stay here for the night?*

What-if's are not bad … but you can go down some rabbit holes with them. Some people believe that what-ifs show a lack of trust in God, because it demonstrates our anxiety and worry about a situation. While this may be technically true, and my what-ifs are most certainly filled with angst and a nonproductive method of trying to cope, there is no amount of Bible verse memorization that is going to stop me from engaging in this behavior, because this is how my mind works—the mind that God gave me and made for me, with a purpose and plan in store for it. Therefore, the trick here is to plan ahead without coming unglued in the process. Somehow rein it in so I come up with ways to potentially approach the Armageddon of my near future, while reminding myself that God is in control and that he is all over this situation. Chill, while also being prepared. It is a delicate line to walk!

It reminds me of a joke my husband tells. There was a man who was in the middle of a flood, and he had crawled out on his roof due to the rising waters. His neighbor comes by in a canoe and offers to take him to safety. The man says, "No, thank you. The Lord will provide." The floodwaters continue to rise, and the National Guard comes along with a rescue boat and tells the man to get in or risk drowning. The man replies, "No, thank you. The Lord will provide." The floodwaters have now overtaken the house, and the man is clinging to his chimney to stay above water. A helicopter comes along, lowers a rope ladder for him to climb up, but the man again states, "No, thank you. The Lord will provide." Shortly thereafter, the man is swept away by the floodwaters and dies. Once he is in heaven, God greets him. The man says, "Lord, I don't understand. I put my full and complete faith that you would provide for me, and you let me perish." The man somehow missed God's provision—the canoe, boat, and helicopter. God was providing all kinds of ways, but sometimes, kid, you have to meet God halfway!

What-ifs aren't all bad. Like most anything in life, moderation is key. There is something to be said for planning ahead, being prepared, gathering your thoughts and resources, and having some contingencies on deck. But we must also remember that God is in control. All those plans you are making, he is making them possible. All those what-ifs—he has got them covered. One of my favorite Bible verses is Psalm 46:10a, "Be still, and know that I am God." I have it on a plaque in my office, on a prayer journal, and even on a bracelet I wear, especially when I need the reminder. So go ahead and plan. Just make sure that you are consulting God along the way and being open to yielding to him as needed.

I'm a visual person, so when I am in the middle of what-ifs, I often have a picture of God in my head (and he looks like the God in *Mighty Python and the Holy Grail* ... that's what having two brothers and no sisters will do for you), looking down at me, shaking his head, saying, "Will you just settle down and breathe for a second? You know I've got this all planned out." And while I do logically know these things, my brain can't seem to be able to throw the off switch on the planning. However, there does seem to be a dimmer switch. Sometimes that is the best we can hope for.

Journal Prompts

1. What are some what-ifs that you struggle with?
2. What kind of planning and thinking did you engage in, and did it help you?
3. What are some Bible verses or biblical truths you remember to keep you grounded?

46

Fear, Worry, and Going Mad

WAITING IS THE WORST

If you ask me what the worst part about cancer is, I will tell you, without hesitation, the waiting. Waiting for the results, to learn how bad your cancer diagnosis is, the prognosis, and what the plan is moving forward. For me, the waiting is when I am the most anxious, and it's usually worse at night. During the daytime, I can keep myself busy and somewhat distracted. Usually, I keep myself so busy that by the time I crawl into bed, I can pray myself to sleep. What a glorious blessing I have been given to usually be able to fall asleep during scary times of the unknown. However, I usually wake up around 2:30 or 3:00 a.m., and that is when I can't sleep, and my mind goes into overdrive. This is also when I am likely to get up and get on the computer and start consulting Dr. Internet. While Dr. Internet can bring some comfort and anxiety relief, mostly what I have found is that I spend a great deal of time reading all kinds of information that contradicts itself, and I am left frustrated, anxious, and not knowing who or what to believe.

What is the best way to deal with the emotional drudgery of waiting? Beats me! I'm not good at waiting, because it seems like such a huge waste of time. It also indicates that I am spoiled, entitled, and selfish. I want what I want (information), and I want it now! I know logically that there are many life and spiritual lessons to be learned in the waiting, but that does little to quell my impatience. Often when I am struggling with waiting, some well-intentioned person will say, "You just have to wait upon the Lord and be patient."

I just smile and say, "You're right. Thank you for that encouragement." While in my head, I'm yelling, "Not helpful! If I knew how to wait and be patient, I wouldn't be struggling right now!" It incensed me that when I was trying to be more successful with waiting, someone would tell me to wait better.

There are, however, some things that I can share with you to ease the waiting—practically and spiritually. First up, as a social worker, I want to impress upon you to be your own medical advocate! Especially in today's health care system. My parents were of the generation that you did not question doctors, and you waited for them to get you your results. Today, medicine is so compartmentalized that it is imperative that you be the liaison between the lab, doctor's office, and medical team. Therefore, you have full and complete permission to be needy—be the squeaky wheel that gets the grease ... within reason. It is perfectly acceptable to call a doctor's office and ask about the status of your test results. Most hospitals and hospital-contracted doctors' offices have online portals where patients' test results are supposed to be posted. This can be good—or very scary. Most of us don't know how to read a lab report or understand the Latin terms that inform medical jargon. Therefore, you can get ahold of a lab report and get yourself all worked up over nothing or decide everything is great when it is most certainly not! Thankfully, in today's medical community, there are so many other people besides the doctor who can talk you through results; you really should not have to wait long once they arrive. Nurses, nurse practitioners, or physician assistants may be able to pitch hit if the doctor is not available.

Furthermore, be nice and polite. You will be amazed at how far you can get with a genuine "please" and "thank you." People in the medical community get very callous to the threats of legal action and general nastiness of patients. We are all like mirrors, usually reflecting back what we receive. Therefore, sincerely nice people can generate a desire for someone to be helpful back. You're going for that "I'll go the extra mile for this patient because they are so nice" reaction from your medical community. There is a reason the saying "you catch more flies with honey than you do vinegar" has been around forever. It's a statement of truth!

Now, spiritually speaking, when it comes to waiting and the horrible holding pattern of the unknown, the best thing I know to do is to throw yourself at the mercy of the Lord and ask for a double dose of peace that passes all understanding. Isaiah must have had some trouble with waiting too, because two great Bible verses on the topic comes from his chapter:

> Yet the Lord longs to be gracious to you; therefore he will rise up to show you compassion. For the Lord is a God of justice. Blessed are all who wait for him! (Isaiah 30:18 NIV)

> But they who wait for the Lord shall renew their strength; they shall mount up with wings like eagles; they shall run and not be weary; they shall walk and not faint. (Isaiah 40:31 ESV)

Here are promises that we are given in his Word. Sometimes he comes through in a big way, and other times, you might feel hung out to dry—but he is there. The way we go about asking is through prayer and working to be in the presence of God. This might mean sitting quietly and reading scripture or looking at specific passages and verses that speak to your situation. Another thing I try to do is to remind myself that God is in control, and my engagement in worry is useless and fruitless. But you know what? I still worry. This is something I struggle with for lots of reasons. But following these steps and focusing on the fact that God has got this helps me to keep it together.

Lastly, seeking out encouragement from others who you know will provide good counsel is also helpful. But the key phrase here is *good counsel*. Someone who has your best interest at heart, not their own. Someone who has some wisdom that they can impart to you. Someone who has been there and done that. It doesn't have to be exactly the same thing, but someone who has been through some adversity and come out the other side in a manner that you would like to emulate.

Journal Prompts

1. Why do you think waiting is difficult?
2. What are some practical things you can do while waiting?
3. What are some spiritual things you can do while waiting?

Fear, Worry, and Going Mad

WHAT IS TAKING SO LONG?

Have you ever heard the saying "Good things come to those who wait"? Or how about "Nothing worthwhile is ever easy," or maybe "Easy is boring"? Well, to these time-honored sayings, I would like to reply, "You know what? I would like to try quick and easy and see for myself!"

It seems like there are several things I have done the long and hard way in my life. I went to college and graduate school before the internet. I remember spending hours in the library doing research in the stacks, sitting in computer labs writing papers because no one had their own personal computer, and toting around dimes and nickels to make copies at the one shared copy machine. When I decided to go back for my PhD, twelve years later, things had changed! I had to teach myself how to use the internet and online learning platforms before I could even start taking classes. I spent four years completing coursework and writing a dissertation, while also raising two young children and working full-time. I did all of this with the hopes of being able to teach at the university level. After I finished my PhD, it took me an additional five years to get hired at my present university. During that time, I taught every adjunct class I was offered in hopes of building my résumé and teaching experience. I published in scholarly journals and presented all over the country at conferences to have more items to add to my curriculum vitae (which is a fancy term for a long résumé). It all paid off in the end. I got hired at the university, and it is the best job

I have ever had. However, while I was working on my PhD, a friend of mine, who was a stay-at-home mom, decided she wanted to be a science teacher. She enrolled in an online course that was designed to be an eighteen-month program, and she finished in in three months. She got a certificate that allowed her to teach grades K–12 and had her dream job before she even passed her nation-wide standardized exam. I remember thinking, *Why is this so quick and easy for her and so long and hard for me?* Patience is not one of my spiritual gifts!

When I was diagnosed with my first cancer, everything went *very quickly.* "You have a lump; let's get an x-ray." I didn't even make it home from the doctor's office before they called and told me I had an appointment with a surgeon because the mass in my clavicle wasn't clear and they were recommending a biopsy. I met with the surgeon, and less than a week later, I had the biopsy. I got my results the next day. I called an oncologist, had my first visit, baseline testing, and first chemo treatment within nine days of diagnosis. My second time around, it seemed like everything took forever! I had to call and advocate for my appointments, for my test results, to get my surgeries scheduled, and to speak with medical professionals when I had complications. I became the squeaky wheel that got the grease … but let me tell you, I had to work for every drop! Test results took several days with in-house labs. Because this was not my first rodeo, I knew that they could get my results faster—you can get blood tests in an hour if you mark them "stat," but not this time around. There were many times when I was waiting for results or to hear from a doctor's office that I could feel myself coming unhinged.

On one occasion, I was out of town at a conference, alone, and literally felt like I had one nerve left—and it was about to give out. I had called the doctor's office multiple times, asked nicely, advocated, begged, and still nothing. Here was the thing that was most maddening. They had my results; just no one had time to give them to me. I was in a breakout session trying to listen to the speaker but was hearing nothing except the blood pumping through my brain as my blood pressure rose while watching my phone for the call. As a means of trying to save my sanity, I pulled out a notebook and started making a list of all the blessings I could. This helped to take the edge off and seemed to ground me a bit. As I made my list, some themes started to present—God was in control. God's timing—in retrospect—was always perfect, and God always provided. I was reminded of Psalm 27:14, which says, "Wait for the Lord; be strong and take heart and wait for the Lord." Was I magically calm and divinely overwhelmed with peace and patience? Absolutely not. I was still a hot mess waiting and so frustrated I could scream (and I did a few times), but I did have a better perspective, which allowed me to wait the time needed until I *finally* got the phone call. It was a long way to go for a minor victory, but it was better than the alternative—taking it out on some poor stranger who just happened to walk into my line of fire and became an easy target, chemically altering myself, or finding some other nonproductive and potentially harmful way of escaping.

Journal Prompts

1. What are two or three positive and productive things you can do when you're feeling like you are about to come emotionally unhinged?
2. How do these activities help you? Why are they magical to you?
3. Why wait until you are having a moment? Engage in one of your activities now for some positive perspective.

Fear, Worry, and Going Mad

IT IS GOING TO TAKE AT LEAST SEVEN MINUTES

I know what my fear/anxiety reaction is. When I get scary or bad news, it hits me right in the gut. My face flushes hot, I have a feeling like my stomach has dropped, and I experience a sense of doom that is palpable. Not to share too much, but I usually end up in the bathroom. I also find myself taking lots of deep, slow breaths. I don't think about it; this just happens. My husband knows what to look for because if I am ever breathing deliberately, he knows I am emotionally uncomfortable. These fear/anxiety-induced experiences are biological reactions, and I have little control over this system kicking in. However, I can do some things to try to get back on top of it. We're gonna get scientific here for a second.

As humans, we are created for survival (yay), but being in survival mode does not feel good. While effective, it is physically and emotionally unpleasant. This is how I try to explain this process to my students: If you're at home watching a movie with your sweetie, you're in the parasympathetic nervous system. You're relaxed, calm, and feeling good. While sitting there on the couch, you might think, *You know, I am a bit snackish. I'd like some popcorn … and I need a bathroom break.* So you pause the movie, put some popcorn in the microwave to pop, and head for the restroom. This is the system that, as humans, we are supposed to live in—all is good, no threats detected, just live your life.

But what happens when you're hiking through the woods and you come across a bear? Instantaneously, you switch from the easygoing parasympathetic nervous system to the sympathetic nervous system. Before you even realize, "Oh no—I'm in trouble!" your body is already in full-alert mode, dumping chemicals into your system to make you as efficient as possible to survive. Your eyes dilate so you can see better, your heart beats faster, and the bronchioles in your lungs open up so you can take more oxygen into your bloodstream to increase your endurance. Other systems that are not needed go offline to divert energy to priority systems. Your digestive system slows down, which is why you will never be running from a bear and think, *Goodness I wish I had a snack right now. I'm a bit peckish.* Additionally, the automatic part of your brain has already chosen how you're going to react, long before your brain has a chance to try to weigh in on the decision. There are four common identified stress reactions:

Fight. The ability to physically defend yourself. You can punch harder, take a hit without feeling it, and your reflexes are catlike sharp. This is also where superhuman strength to lift cars off people comes from.

Flight. Get out of Dodge. Just book it and don't look in the rearview mirror. You can run faster and longer than you normally could.

Freeze. Become as small and nonthreatening as possible. Contrary to widely held belief, this is not a bad reaction style. This stance helps to ensure the least amount of damage with an event that can't be stopped.

Fawn. Making nice with the attacker and working to placate their needs to avoid damage, hurt, or pain.

It's important to remember that you do not get to pick your reaction. When humans are in survival mode, the parts of the brain that are in overdrive are making decisions before the logical part of the brain catches up, which is a good thing. In the midst of a life-threatening crisis, you don't want to be comparing the pros and cons of each stress reaction. The problem is lots of people don't know this, and after an event has passed, they start to reflect on what happened. Often, they start to criticize their reaction and wish they had handled things differently. All kinds of thinking errors can start to set up camp. The system does what the system needs to do to survive.

While the human survival system works well, sometimes it can work too well. Anyone who has ever had a panic attack knows this. For whatever reason, the survival system has kicked in, and the sympathetic nervous system has been switched on. All those chemicals are flowing, and once this system starts, even if you can convince yourself that this is a false alarm and there is no need for concern, it will take a minimum of seven minutes for the chemicals to move their way through the body. That means that even if you can logically identify that you are not in danger, you are going to be physically uncomfortable for a bit.

Because the high alert switch is in our brain, this is also where the off switch is located. Therefore, to get yourself back to normal, you have to intentionally engage in some cognitive and physical behaviors to get the survival system to shut down. Then you must wait for the chemicals to flush through. Knowing all this information is *very* helpful; making yourself breathe slowly further communicates to the brain that everything is okay—you can just settle down now. But the real trick is keeping your wits about you while you wait for the system to reset. It's not going to feel great, but it will pass! In times like this, it's vital to have a reset plan. A list of things that work for you. This is more than just biology; this is a recommendation for God as well. Proverbs 4:23 says, "Above all else, guard your heart, for everything you do flows from it." Actions that signal to your brain to hit the off switch. Behaviors and cognitions you can engage in for the next several minutes until you feel better. Here are some ideas, but ultimately, you must figure out what works for you.

- *Just breathe.* There are lots of breathing techniques out there. The main goal here is to slow your breathing to communicate to the brain that there is no need for alarm.
- *Pray*—always a good one. Let the peace that comes from your connection with God calm you. Even if you aren't feeling that peace that passes all understanding, reminding yourself that God is in control can help a great deal.
- *Be active.* Some people like to walk or jog, while others like to run full out or engage in a hard workout. Activity can help to counteract the survival chemicals with feel-good exercise chemicals.

- *Get your mind on something else* through reading, music, and/or visual mediums. Just be careful to pick encouraging and positive entertainment. Remember—junk in, junk out.
- *Complete a body inventory.* Intentionally check each part of your body. Most people like to start with the feet and move up.
- *Journal, write, or color.* Some people like to write out what is going on. It slows down your brain because you can't write as fast as you think. Other people enjoy adult coloring books. These create anxiety for me, but if they work for you, go for it.
- *Spend some time with a pet.*
- *Rock something*—a baby, toddler, pet, or just yourself. There is a reason babies like to be rocked; it's comforting.
- *Engage in a mind activity*—like a cognitive puzzle, word find, or listing the states alphabetically.
- *Be intentional.* Do something positive and allow it to work. Nothing changes if you don't change something.

Journal Prompts

1. What are five things you can do when you feel panicky, fearful, or anxious to help reset your system faster? Why do you think these listed items work for you?
2. Why is it so hard to engage in these things when we are in the middle of something difficult?

49

Fear, Worry, and Going Mad

HISSY FITS AND ACTING OUT
ARE ALLOWED ... FOR A WHILE

I can usually keep it together, or at least hide enough of what emotional outrage is brewing until I can get to a safe space and really let down and say what I am thinking, uncensored. Often, this is me in my bathroom mirror. No one hears it except me and the Lord—who I picture shaking his head and saying, "Now, Dana ... my goodness child. Some perspective please!" Rarely is it helpful or productive, but I have spent hours saying to the mirror what I would love to honestly say to someone else but would never dare to breathe aloud, for fear of negative consequences or hurting someone to the core.

It took me a long time to admit that I was angry with God concerning my second go-around with cancer. In my mind, it was arrogant, wrong, and dangerous, not to mention very un-Christian like. I also thought it was sinful, and I feared making God angry with me. I was in no position to bite the hand that feeds me. When I watch action movies and it is certain that someone is about to die a gruesome death, and the character lets out a slur of curse words, I always think, *Oof—do you want to be cursing right now, right before you are about to meet your Maker? Maybe if you didn't curse so much, you might get some much-needed divine intervention.* Because that's it. I didn't want to admit that I was mad at God and risk decreasing the help that he might provide in my situation.

Now, I know that this is absurd for a number of reasons. First, there is no need to hide anything from God, because he knows everything I'm thinking. While I might have been trying to spin it in all kinds of other directions, God knew what I was dealing with. Second, anger doesn't scare God. I have told many friends and clients this very thing, but then it came to me that I couldn't seem to take my own advice. I sure didn't want to admit this to the people in my life, because it was embarrassing and felt childish. Additionally, I didn't want others to know what I was already thinking about myself: *you're a bad Christian if you don't accept God's will for your life.* Third, anger is a God-given emotion, so there is a reason for it. Perhaps working through the anger is where the growth is. The complicating factor is that anger doesn't resolve quickly or easily. Additionally, once you start diving into it, you tend to find lots of other unsavory things that are keeping this unpleasantness going.

So how do you know if you are angry with God? Just like if you are angry at anyone else that you feel pressure to hide—it comes out in your actions, words, and worldview. The first time I had an ah-ha moment concerning my anger with God was in my office. After learning that I had breast cancer, they found a slightly enlarged lymph node in my armpit. Therefore, it had to be biopsied to see if the cancer had spread. If the lymph node was positive, that automatically meant the stage of cancer I had would be moving up, and the higher the stage, the worse the prognosis. I also knew that lymph node involvement most certainly meant chemo and radiation. I was waiting for my biopsy results, and we have already discussed how bad I am at waiting, when I snapped. Alone, in my office, at God. I was whisper-screaming at God, "Enough already. I know that with a wave of your hand, you can make anything happen. And I am here to tell you I am tired of waiting. It isn't fair that I have to do this again, so the least you could do is get me my test results in a timely fashion so I know what I am facing." I was on my feet, stomping, crying, and blowing snot, and I meant every word of what I was saying. I knew beyond a shadow of a doubt that God could make my phone ring right then and there, and my results would be provided. And because I knew he could do it, and it wasn't happening, that God was making me wait … *on purpose!* "No, sir—no more! Whatever lesson you have to teach me, you are going to have to do it another way because I have had enough of this. You need to make this phone ring with good news …

right now!" That's right, reader. I was telling God what he needed to do for me. I was like an impudent child having a hissy fit in my office. It must have looked ridiculous—a forty-nine-year-old woman, trained social worker, university professor, trauma therapist who claimed to be a Christian … on the verge of lying down on the floor, kicking her feet, and holding her breath until she got what she wanted.

So … did my phone ring? Nope. Did I feel God's comfort and peace? Nope. Did I respond with faith that God had a reason for this trial in my life? Nope. Did I crawl into the Word and try to find some wisdom and God-breathed direction? Nope. I cursed God and said, "Fine … I'm on my own here, eh? What's new! No problem, God. I'm a veteran of this cancer stuff, right? Go ahead, sit this one out—I got it." I dried my face, set my mind to work, and began to suffer in silence and isolation. How could I ever tell anyone of this exchange? I was truly on my own … and in trouble … and it was of my own doing. I had gotten mad at God—the *Lord Almighty*—now! The creator of all things, the author of all my many blessings, my provider who had come through in all things in the past, the maker of my children. I had gone and lost my temper with the one person you are not allowed to be angry with. The one who is in control, the one who holds my fate in his hands, the one who has the master plan in place. And now, I will be rewarded with nothing. No peace or sense of his presence. And who could blame him?

Do you see my monumental mistake here? I had given God human qualities. I decided that God responded to me the way I would have responded if someone had treated me with such contempt and disdain. And because I struggle with forgiving others when they really hurt me, and I tend to cut people off emotionally when I am wounded, then God would certainly not be hanging around to see what I needed next. I imagined God looking down at me saying, "You spoiled, ungrateful brat. You think you have it so tough. You have no idea the tragedy that I could rein down on you. You think you have problems; you got nothing compared to other people. So, you know what, kid? Just see what it feels like to try to wander through this valley alone. You want to do it yourself? Have at it." Again … this is how Dana Branson would have responded; this is *not* how God responds … thank goodness! But in that time, I was so wrapped up in my anger, frustration, and anxiety that it fit my worldview. And like so many things that are not true but creations of our own cognitive making that spill over into our perception, there were plenty of other things happening that reinforced my thinking errors into my reality.

Looking back now, I can see where I went off the rails. I can see how my emotions were driving my boat into dangerous and dark waters … and then I got lost out there for a while. If I could have just swallowed my pride and talked with someone, I would not have stayed out there so long. If I had reevaluated my perceptions with Psalm 138:8, "The Lord will fulfill his purpose for me; your steadfast love, O Lord, endures forever. Do not forsake the work of your hands" (EVS), I could have turned my boat around sooner. I might have been able to see that God was waiting with his arms wide open, saying, "I have been here the whole time, child. You are never getting rid of me because you are mine, for all eternity. I forgive, and I forget. Please allow my truth to be your truth and to vanquish these lies you have been listening to for too long."

Journal Prompts

1. What are the lies you hear sometimes in your own mind?
2. What is God's truth about those lies?

Fear, Worry, and Going Mad

UNHELPFUL AND NONPRODUCTIVE—
BUT I CAN'T STOP!

As a Christian, social worker, and someone who has been through cancer more than once, I recognize and realize that unhelpful and nonproductive thinking is movement in the wrong direction. I know logically that it leads to nowhere good, stalls progress, and eventually you either have to adjust your thinking and get out of that mess, or it will turn you into a bitter person. I also know, logically, that you can't hide this. The longer you hold on to and hang out with unhelpful and nonproductive thinking, the more it builds up and spills over onto other things in your life, like relationships, work, interactions with strangers, frustration tolerance, and your overall worldview. You may have met some of these people in your life, or you might fear that you are becoming one yourself. People do not want to be around embittered people. They are like succubi; they drain the life out of others.

I would love to tell you that I did not struggle with unproductive and bitter thoughts because I rose above all of it with my focus on God's love and provision and my intentionality. However, I can't. It's embarrassing, but I started down this road … and got much further than I ever thought I would. There are lots of reasons why, many of which I have discussed at length in these devotions. One of the biggest reasons is that I stopped talking to people. I tried to deal with the aftermath of a second cancer and the negative emotions it brought by myself, and I allowed lots and lots and lots of unhelpful and nonproductive thinking to set up camp in my mind. Although it was unhealthy, there is something seductive about thinking errors. Much like a succubus, you are pulled in before you know it. For months, I was utterly convinced that no one cared—that I was so insignificant that no one noticed me. And during this time, on numerous occasions, someone would say something insensitive that I would take as proof of my thinking errors. Like when people at church, where I had been a member for more than twenty-five years, would come up to me and my husband (who has always been the popular extrovert in our coupling) and say something like this:

> "Excuse me, can you wait to talk with Dr. Branson until I am done?"
> "Oh, I'm sorry. I'm his wife. I didn't mean to be inconsiderate."
> "Really? You are? I've never noticed you before."

One morning, during the welcome portion of worship when you are supposed to shake hands with people, I received this:

> "Hey, girl, you coming back to church?"
> "Ah … no, I'm here every Sunday."
> "Oh, my bad. I see Alan all the time but never you."

In the past, I had this conversation:

> "Hi, my name is Amber (not her real name). Is this your first time at our Bible study?"
> "No, I've been coming for several weeks now."
> "Oh, I've never noticed you. Where do you go to church?"
> "Same church as you."
> "No kidding. Really? I've never seen you before. Are you married?"
> "Yes, I'm married to Alan Branson."
> "Really? That is so funny. We have an Alan Branson at our church."

"Yes, I know. He's my husband."

"No, no—this Alan Branson is a deacon at our church."

"Yes, I know. That's my husband."

"No, no—this Alan Branson is an eye doctor in town."

"Yes, I know. That's my husband."

"No, no—the Alan Branson I'm talking about plays with our worship team sometimes."

"Yes, I know. That's my husband. He plays the banjo."

"Well, girl, you need to be coming to church and worshiping with your man."

"I do—every Sunday. I sit right beside him!"

"I don't think so, or I would have seen you."

No lie. This was a real conversation I had with a person from my church. What was her message to me? *You can't possibly be married to Alan Branson. He is wonderful, and you are clearly not worthy enough for him.* Unfortunately, I have experienced several encounters like this. My husband can attest to it. He shakes his head and says, "I don't understand it." In my head, what I hear from these encounters is, "No one sees you because you are insignificant, you are not deserving, and no one wants you around." You carry this thinking around for a while, it does stuff to you. When I felt small, I became small, and after a while, I started to believe that no one cared … not even God. I once told my husband that I should make my anonymity work for me and become a criminal.

Stuff like this makes it easy to get wrapped up in unhelpful and nonproductive thinking, like a blanket. The problem is, if left unchecked, this blanket becomes a cocoon, and out of it is hatched someone you do not want to be. A person who doesn't realize how unappealing they are to be around and how hurtful their words and comments can be to others. Luke 6:45 says, "A good man brings good things out of the good stored up in his heart, and an evil man brings evil things out of the evil stored up in his heart. For the mouth speaks what the heart is full of." Best to jump on unhelpful and nonproductive thinking as soon as it starts, or you risk becoming what you are entertaining in your mind. No one, including you, wants that!

Journal Prompts

1. What are some unhelpful and nonproductive thoughts you carry around with you?
2. Why are they unhelpful and nonproductive? What is carrying them around doing for you?
3. What is some truth you can replace this thinking with? What would God say to you about his creation in you?

Author's Note

Now what? I hope that the last devotion you read was not the one directly before this page. If so, you haven't ended on a very happy note. The good stuff is at the beginning of the book, and the harder stuff is at the end. But if you read the introduction, you know that this book was meant to be read more like a menu than cover to cover. Pick what you need or want for the day. Therefore, if you have ended on "Fear, Worry, and Going Mad," I would strongly encourage you to find a more joyful, inspiring devotion to review.

Adversity can be a beast—a sneaky, sly, unpredictable animal that can show up when you least expect it. Or it can be a phenomenon that launches you to the best version of yourself. I sincerely hope that you are experiencing the latter. This book took me over a year to write, and I feel like I went through all the emotions on the journey of creating it. Then I got to revisit a lot of those same emotions in the process of preparing the book for print. Adversity and grief are like waves in the ocean. Sometimes the waves are big and close together, and they come crashing in, bringing destruction in their path and making a royal mess of things. In time, the waves get smaller and spread out, and the damage is less and less. But remember, adversity is sneaky. Out of nowhere, you can be hit with a big wave. I like to think this is the adversity beast reminding you that it is still around and capable of taking you places you don't want to go. This is also why we must continue to do those things that keep us in a good place. It is like walking up a descending escalator; the moment we stop focusing on God's Word, his promises, and being intentional in our thoughts and actions, we put ourselves in danger of heading to a place we don't want to go. A place of stinking thinking, pity pot, and negativity. It can take a long time to crawl out of this place and feel good again, but sliding back happens quickly. Be intentional and purposeful, and surround yourself with the right people, places, and playthings to ensure you stay where you need to be … or don't. It is your choice, and sometimes we choose to visit the most unhelpful places. Perhaps a visit every once in a while is what you need to be reminded of why this is not how you want to live your life. Just don't hang out there too long, friend. You know what you need to do, and you know how to do it. Take charge and take on the mindset you want … or at least fake it till it sticks. Sometimes we do that too.

I will leave you one last verse, my personal favorite, Joshua 1:9: "Be strong and courageous. Do not be afraid; do not be discouraged, for the Lord your God will be with you *wherever* [emphasis added] you go." Wherever means wherever—physically, cognitively, emotionally, and spiritually. God is there, even when your stuff is interfering with your ability to see, feel, or even believe. When you try to push him away because you don't want him around, God is there. And when you come to your senses and rejoice that he didn't leave, God holds no record of wrong; he just delights in you and your worship of all he is.

Bibliography

Ebert, A. "Kennesaw Mountain: Canine Mascots of the Civil War." National Park Service, US Department of the Interior. https://www.nps.gov/kemo/learn/historyculture/upload/Canine-Mascots-bulletin_A.pdf.

Livestrong. "Second Cancers," 2021. https://www.livestrong.org/we-can-help/healthy-living-after-treatment/second-cancers.

Loughead, F. H. "Footprints in the Sand." *Evening Star*, January 2, 1892.

Smith-Barusch, A. *Foundations of Social Policy: Social Justice in Human Perspective.* 6th ed. Cengage, 2018.

Tedeschi, R. G., and L.G. Calhoun. "The Posttraumatic Growth Inventory: Measuring the Positive Legacy of Trauma." *Journal of Trauma Stress* 9, no. 3 (1996): 455–471. https://doi.org/10.1007/BF02103658.

About the Author

Dana C. Branson is the wife of Alan and mom to Anna Judith "AJ" and Noah—two gifts of grace—and mother-in-law to Jesus-loving Isaac, who makes her daughter's heart go pitter-patter. She is a professor of social work at Southeast Missouri State University. Before teaching full-time, she was a practicing licensed clinical social worker, with more than twenty-five years of experience with substance-use disorders, mental health, co-occurring disorders, and trauma-informed care. Dana has a PhD in psychology, a master's of social work, and a bachelor's of science in psychology and sociology. She regularly serves as a conference presenter discussing vicarious and secondary traumas, adverse childhood events (ACE), substance-use disorder topics, the importance of school social workers, and a variety of other topics. Dana has also had the privilege of participating in international social work opportunities in Ireland, Brazil, and Belarus. When not grading papers or trying to write for publications as a professor, she enjoys walking, snuggling on the couch with her husband and watching movies, and traveling. She has an affinity for Scotland, Hamish Macbeth, and Southwest Baptist University—go Bearcats! She is also an honorary roadie/groupie for the musical talents of her banjo-playing husband.